Employees Gone WILD

Employees Gone WILD

CRAZY (AND TRUE!) STORIES OF OFFICE MISBEHAVIOR AND WHAT YOU CAN LEARN FROM THE MISTAKES OF OTHERS

Richard Burton, Esq.

with illustrations by Ian Baker

Skyhorse Publishing

Skyhorse Publishing books may be purchased in bulk at special discounts for sales promotion, corporate gifts, fund-raising, or educational purposes. Special editions can also be created to specifications. For details, contact the Special Sales Department, Skyhorse Publishing, 307 West 36th Street, 11th Floor, New York, NY 10018 or info@skyhorsepublishing.com.

Visit our website at www.skyhorsepublishing.com.

10 9 8 7 6 5 4 3 2 1

Library of Congress Cataloging-in-Publication Data is available on file.

Cover design by Owen Corrigan

Cover and interior illustrations by Ian Baker

Print ISBN: 978-1-63220-633-6

Ebook ISBN: 978-1-63220-779-1

Printed in the United States of America

TABLE OF CONTENTS

INTRODUCTION

Imagine if you will the following workplace scenarios:

- Two employees having hot and heavy sex in an open cubicle in full view of coworkers.
- An employee leaving a special deposit in the bathroom paper towel dispenser.
- A fired employee texting her former boss to threaten suicide.
- Police showing up at the office and dragging an employee away in handcuffs.
- Oral sex solicitations via office e-mail.

Impossible? Unbelievable?

Astonishingly, all these, and other equally outrageous scenarios, are real. I was there.

Read on. The scandalous details are all in these pages.

I'm an attorney with over twenty years of legal and business experience. I've served as general counsel for more than fifteen different corporations, acting through a handful of holding companies. A major part of my job has been overseeing human resources investigations. In the course of conducting and managing over one hundred cases, I've become privy to shocking behavior among employees and management, ranging from the idiotic to the bizarre to the flat-out criminal.

Because, while they're happening, HR investigations are strictly confidential, I've never shared my knowledge of what goes on behind the scenes at the average office and how crazy things can actually get . . . until now. (Don't worry. The names have been changed to protect the innocent—and the guilty!)

Each chapter of *Employees Gone Wild* covers a different area of, shall we say, colorful workplace behavior, illustrated with vivid examples drawn from my own case files, and occasionally supplemented with equally colorful stories from the experience of colleagues and business associates. The place you work is crazy? Let's see if you can top what I've seen. (No, don't take that as a challenge. Please.)

Why share all these wild and woolly workplace adventures? Well, it's not to give employees ideas. You'll note that most of the perpetrators paid a price for their behavior, ranging from disciplinary action to firing to arrest and jail time.

What I would like to give you in this book, along with a roller-coaster ride of hilarious workplace craziness, is some good business and personal advice, whether you're a rank-and-file employee, a supervisor or manager, or a human resources professional. We can all learn from the experiences of these employees from hell. What I am not here to give you (warning: a typical disclaimer from a lawyer is coming) is any form of legal advice.[1]

More times than I can count, employees called on the carpet for some egregious misdeed have claimed they didn't know what they were doing was wrong. Yeah, sure, some of them were lying. But I am confident that a lot of the bafflement was genuine. It's true that many of us are thrust from school straight into the workplace with nothing but observation to

[1] No legal opinions or advice are given in this book. In addition, no attorney-client relationship is formed or intended to be formed by any of the content contained in this book.

tell us what is okay and what is not—and depending where you work, the examples around you might not be the best ones. There are also a lot of fuzzy lines: we spend a lot of hours at work, so our relationships and activities there may bleed into the personal, and vice versa.

Throughout this book, I've included guidance on where to draw lines between personal and professional, what kind of things are appropriate in what kind of workplace, where to get help if you find yourself harassed or discriminated against, and what will happen and how to handle yourself if you do get into trouble. Think of it as a short—but undeniably entertaining—course on how to keep your job and build a career—and what you should definitely not do.

For managers, supervisors, and human resources professionals, I've included memos to management with thoughts on how to spot trouble, how to nip that trouble in the bud, and how to address it after the fact. Rank-and-file employees can benefit from that info, too: think of it as a peek inside your boss's head and make it your edge to get ahead.

Let's start with a little basic information.

Frequently Unasked Questions aka Things You Never Asked, But Should

What is a Human Resources Department for?

> Despite popular opinion, they're not just there to screen résumés and send out memos about policies and rules.
>
> Back in the olden days, they were called personnel departments; the name change was intended to recognize that people are the most important resource in any company. No matter how good your product or service, you

won't succeed if the people producing and delivering it aren't doing quality work.

Human resources departments deal with everything from hiring (where most of us get to know them) to evaluating employee performance, training and developing staff, helping managers get the best out of their employees, overseeing employee benefits and workplace conditions, making sure pay and benefits are equitable, managing organizational change, and solving problems that involve people (which is pretty much any kind of problem). When those problems become extreme, the HR department will be involved with the remedy, especially when it includes firing somebody.

If the only time you deal with them is when something bad is happening, yes, they will seem like the company cops. And there are good and bad HR people, just like in every other job.

So you're a lawyer. Are there usually lawyers in HR? Because that seems kind of . . . excessive.

Nope. I'm in a completely separate department; human resources professionals have their own special set of skills. But a lawyer may become involved any time the situation has legal ramifications for the company: when the company might get in trouble because of something an employee has done; when someone is being fired (for instance, in case they decide to sue—the lawyer's job is to make sure the company doesn't break any laws and open the door to legal or financial liability); when a contract is being negotiated and signed; and of course, when the police are or might be involved (companies are just like the perps on *Law & Order* in that regard: they want their lawyer).

I might get involved earlier than lawyers at some other companies because I work for a large company that has in-house legal people and because I have a lot of experience with HR issues, so the HR professionals may stop by my office for advice or help whenever a novel problem arises.

When do the regular HR people get involved?

That varies. A manager may bring them into the conversation when an employee problem exceeds his or her ability to solve, or they feel an impartial third party would help the situation. Some managers bring HR in because they want someone else to be the bad guy. (See how HR people get that reputation?) Managers are just as likely as other employees to land on the HR department's top-secret Bane of Our Existence list.

Employees might come to HR if they don't feel comfortable talking to their bosses about problems, or if the problem is with the boss. Good HR people also keep an ear to the ground and may discover a potential problem early enough to nip it in the bud.

HR is frequently involved in any kind of problem involving substance use/abuse because of the risks to both people and company from alcohol and drug use on the job. Similarly, HR is brought into the picture immediately in cases of sexual harassment.

I am a model employee. What kind of people aren't?

Of course you are a model employee. (You can decide whether I'm giving you the side-eye or not.) Problem employees come from all departments, all levels in the organization, all ages and races and sexes. But in general, there are probably more issues, in my experience, with younger employees, those who may not have learned yet what is or isn't appropriate in the workplace, especially when large groups of young people work together without guidance and mentoring from more mature staff. If a department is like a college dorm or frat house, well, it's not that surprising if people start acting like teenagers away from home for the first time.

Not to say young people have a monopoly on going wild by any means. You'll see in the stories in this book that *Animal House* behavior knows no boundaries.

What can my company fire me for?

Laws regarding hiring and firing vary from state to state. There may also be union contracts or industry standards and regulations that come into play, depending on your job and field. But if you do anything illegal, it will be hard for you to hold on to your job. And if you do anything that damages the company's business, you're on very thin ice.

But you're the model employee. You would never do anything like that. You're not anything like the people in this book. Right?

The people in this book set the bar for wild workplace behavior pretty high—and then cleared that bar with inches to spare. If you haven't decided on a career and want one with lots of variety and a new challenge every day, not to mention a never-ending supply of crazy stories, you might want to consider a career in human resources. The downside? You have to deal with employee behavior like the stories in the pages that follow.

So let's go wild.

And let the craziness begin!

CHAPTER 1

Walks of Shame

Office Sexcapades and the Ugly Morning After

It's no secret that office work can be tedious. Long days spent in seemingly endless yet unproductive meetings. Lonely hours sequestered in a joyless cubicle. The torments of rush-hour traffic. Lunch hours spent eating microwaved leftovers at your desk. Coffee breaks and trips to the water cooler that somehow fail to make the end of the business day seem even one second closer.

The monotony of the nine-to-five routine can feel claustrophobic, even soul crushing. Little wonder some office workers try to spice up their days by flirting with colleagues. And some of them, as you're about to see, take that flirtation a step—or a giant leap—further.

CASE FILE

If the Cubicle Is Rocking, Don't Come Knocking

Let's start with an extreme example, a cautionary tale for the ages. It was a Friday afternoon in July at Company X . . . or perhaps I should call it Company XXX. Most employees were attending a company-sponsored picnic, but a few workers, for whatever reason, had skipped the event to put in a full day at the office. While the rest of the office were enjoying hamburgers and hot dogs and participating in morale-building activities, two employees back at the office were engaging in what you might call an immoral-building activity.

The following Monday, a female employee who had stayed at the office on Friday turned up in the HR department to report that she remembered nothing from about three o'clock that Friday afternoon until about four-thirty on Saturday morning—when she woke up in a jail cell.

Not your usual Monday morning in HR. But the story is far from over.

We learned on investigating that, upon leaving work, the woman had driven to a local hotel where she behaved in an erratic fashion—enough that the hotel staff didn't want to deal with her. The hotel called her a cab. The cab driver said she was incoherent, acting "drunk"—more than the usual drunk needing a ride home on a Friday night. He phoned the police, who arrested her for disorderly conduct. Hence the jail cell.

Did any of her coworkers notice anything unusual on Friday before she left work? Oh yes, they did.

This employee worked in a floor of cubicles with little or no privacy. A colleague, a new employee who was closing her first sale, reported going to the jailbird employee to ask a question. A male coworker was massaging the woman's neck as she sat at her desk responding to the inquiry.

The new staffer came back a short time later with another question. Now the guy's hands were down the front of the woman's blouse. Apparently unfazed, they answered her question.

The third time she stopped by the woman's cube, the newbie found her mentor with her blouse completely off and the male coworker kneading her breasts.

"HOLD ON A SECOND... I JUST HAVE TO SIGN THIS JOB OFF FIRST..."

They still answered her questions—the business questions. Not the ones undoubtably on her mind: What kind of place is this? What have I got myself into, working here?

And the fourth time, the clothes were off, and the woman and her colleague were having sex on the desk. In a cubicle. In plain view.

They barely paused to answer her question.

I know what you're thinking: Did the young woman manage to close the deal?

Oh, that's not what you're wondering? Yes, other people saw the tumescent twosome in action. In fact, when questioned, we learned that *everyone* who was in the office that Friday afternoon had gotten a good look at the action. As I said, it was an open office, and they weren't exactly discreet.

Then things went from bizarre to disturbing.

The woman told HR that, before the turn of events the junior staffer (and everyone else) had witnessed, the man involved had given her an alcoholic drink and insisted that she try it. Because she had no memory of anything that happened afterward, she believed she had been drugged.

I immediately launched a full HR investigation. I interviewed the woman who had brought the complaint, the employees who had witnessed the scene, and finally the man in question. Both the man and woman involved were married to different people and both had children.

The male employee rather sheepishly admitted bringing alcohol to the office and giving his female coworker a drink, but he vehemently denied drugging her. He did, however, admit to having sex with her in front of others, explaining, in what may be the understatement of the year, that things had gotten "out of hand." He apologized and begged for his job, assuring us that if we let him stay he would have no more contact of any kind with any female employee.

Needless to say, we fired him on the spot. The woman involved chose not to pursue any legal or criminal action.

After the Morning After

Bad enough to lose your job for getting busy—and I mean that in the nonwork way—at the workplace. What happens afterward, when looking for another job? Can or should a prior employer reveal what really happened if asked for a reference?

Labor and employment laws have grown much more proemployee over the years, putting companies at serious risk of legal claims if they say or do too much. For this reason, most companies reveal only "name, rank, and employment dates" when anyone inquires about a former employee. If a company were to communicate forthrightly to a third party what it believes an employee may or may not have done, that company would be opening itself to legal claims, with all the attendant expense and bad publicity. (However, if the woman in this situation had taken the man to court, the company would have the public record of that case to fall back on.) And even if the company said nothing, that court record would have followed the man to his next potential job. Is a one-afternoon stand really worth it?

Situations like this are often very tricky for companies to navigate. As far as a company's "need" to do more, in many situations like this, companies simply don't know for sure if a crime has been committed. HR departments may be the dress code and time clock cops, but they aren't the police, with subpoenas or search warrants. It is often one person's word against another's, and that's all there is to go on. Here, for example, it was impossible to know for sure who was telling the truth. Even if the woman had evidence of the presence of a date-rape drug, the company had no right to demand this information, and the woman didn't offer it. The company had no standing to file a criminal complaint against the male employee at issue. The female employee could have, but she decided not to.

The man was fired for breaking company rules; that's always within the company's power. The woman, too, had likely violated company policy, but because of the possibility she was indeed drugged and therefore not in control of or responsible for her actions, she was not fired. Though we did not know for certain that she had been drugged, neither could we prove she wasn't. On balance, and based on her prior employment record, we decided to give her the benefit of the doubt. Still, the situation was enough that she quit two weeks later and moved out of state.

TIPS
Office Sex

- If you must have sex with a coworker, wait until you can get off-site. If you get caught having sex in the workplace, embarrassment might be the least of your worries. There are very few jobs, other than porn star, where sex in the office is not a violation of company policy, and one you almost always will be fired for.
- If you *really* can't wait, find an empty storage room or closet or something. Keep it on the down low. Nobody at the office needs to see the two of you in the act. (Nobody at work needs to see you undressed, under any circumstances, unless you are a nude model by profession. Do you really want to hear people talking about the mole on your back-side at the water cooler?)

- Make sure everyone involved is a fully consenting adult. If there is alcohol involved, consent may be in question. (And should you really be drinking in the office without permission? That's a whole 'nother subject.) Same for drugs. If there's a question of consent, there's a question of legality. Instead of explaining yourself to Human Resources, you may be facing the police and a judge.

MEMO TO MANAGEMENT

Sexual misconduct in the workplace can be a minefield. A swift, thorough, and impartial investigation by HR is essential in limiting the potential damage that such out-of-control employee behavior can wreak upon a company. It is equally, if not more, essential to act decisively in accordance with established protocol and to seek legal advice specific to the facts and circumstances, once the investigation is concluded.

CASE FILE
Cougar on the Prowl

Male employees are not the only ones guilty of sexual misbehavior. One recently divorced middle-aged female employee developed a sudden interest in young male employees. This "cougar"—let's call her Kat[2]—used office email to approach these young male gazelles.

When this was brought to our attention, we warned Kat that we would be monitoring her emails. She seemed to have gotten the message at first, but months later, when a

[2] No real names are used in this book.

" HELLO, CUTIE-PIE.... I'M THE PERK OF THE JOB!.."

twenty-year-old man was hired, she began to email him to ask questions—such as the color of his boxers—and to invite him to meet her in a quiet part of the office so she could "feel his body up." Incredibly, this woman even warned the man in question to be careful in his replies, "because the company told me they might be monitoring emails." (She was not employed as a rocket scientist.)

Since she had disregarded our clear warning and resumed her bad email habits, we had no choice but to fire her. In this case, the new male employee—who had proved unable to resist temptation—got off, so to speak, with a stern warning but was not terminated.

TIPS

X-Ray Vision

- Don't fool yourself by thinking that company emails, text messages, or any other correspondence on company time or devices are private. They're company property, and yes, management can look at whatever you write. (Not just sexual advances—that screed against your boss might pop up to haunt you, too.)
- Same goes for anything you put in a memo or say out loud. Behave at work as though you're being monitored all the time. Big Brother may not always be watching, but you can never be sure.

MEMO TO MANAGEMENT

Employees may be adults, but that doesn't mean they will always act that way. In the immortal words of President Ronald Reagan: "Trust but verify."

CASE FILE
Not-So-Private Message

For a time, it seemed that inappropriate sexual behavior was spreading through Company XXX like the kind of disease you don't want to admit to having. What's more likely, of course, is that email and other electronic messaging systems have made it easier for companies to discover the evidence, even long after the affair is over. Such incriminating recorded behavior has been the undoing of many employees.

What triggered our investigation this time were complaints about a female employee, Tessie, who was whiling away her workdays flirting with numerous coworkers. While examining her in-house instant messages, we stumbled on a bigger problem.

One of Tessie's correspondents, Tom, wasn't just talking dirty to Tessie on the company's systems.

We found a lot of evidence proving Tom was spending his days instant-messaging female coworkers, inviting them to his office during the day for assignments other than work. Unfortunately, he had several takers. Or should I say "givers."

TIPS
Digital Don'ts

- All those emails and instant messages and anything else on your computer? It's all backed up. You may think you deleted that incriminating email or ill-conceived text, but the backup is forever. Think before you type. Your message is for the ages.
- If you want to have private communication with coworkers, do it through private channels—your personal device

and account, sent to the other party's personal device and account. If the other person doesn't want to share his or her email address or cell number, maybe you should take a hint.

A surprising number of women took Tom up on the offer. In fact, the message trail indicated that the action was taking place in his office not just on an almost daily basis, but in some cases, several times during a single day!

Did I mention that Tom's manager shared an office wall with this workplace Casanova? Apparently, the office had good sound insulation because the manager never caught on.

While Tom had the good sense to keep his trysts behind closed doors, and all parties were consenting adults (we had the correspondence to prove it), this is still not what a company means when they encourage good employee relations.

And there was one interaction that put all the others to shame.

The messages showed us that Tom had invited a recently hired female employee to one of his very private meetings. She responded to his attempted seduction by telling him that she knew he was married and she was not interested in involving herself with a married man. His reply, and I quote: "In that case, I would just need to rape you—haha."

The woman to whom this "joke" was addressed did not report it to HR. She did, however, leave her job soon afterward for a better-paying position.

In fact, no one had ever complained about this man officially. His adventures only came to light because of the complaints about Tess.

When Tom was called on the carpet for his threat to sexually assault a coworker, he insisted that he had only been joking. We weren't laughing. He was fired.

As I escorted him out of the office, he said, "Welcome to a day in my life—women are always throwing themselves at me!"

TIPS

Advance and Retreat

- If you're on the receiving end of an unwanted advance at the workplace, report the incident to your supervisor or HR manager. There are rules against this, and it's up to management to stop it.
- Even if an employee attempts to laugh off his or her advances as a joke, if you feel at all uncomfortable or threatened, report the incident to HR. It's *not* okay for coworkers to make you feel uncomfortable in this way.
- On the other hand, if it is a "wanted" advance, arrange for the tryst to happen off company premises and after hours. What you do on your own time is up to you.

MEMO TO MANAGEMENT

It is not enough to have policies about harassment in place. Employees must know and understand them. Wise and prudent management will ensure that all employees understand what company policy is and what steps they should take to protect themselves—and the company—from scandal, liability, and worse.

CASE FILE
Leather Barred

Company XXX wasn't alone. At a different company, a high-level male executive was extremely proud of the posh leather couch in his office. All that talk about the couch, which wasn't just about the status symbol, but also had a nudge-nudge-wink-wink tone to it, led to rumors—rumors about what our executive, Ken, was doing on office furniture. I heard from my assistant that the talk was that Ken was conducting after-hours hanky-panky with certain female employees.

There were names attached to the rumors, which meant I could follow up. I talked to two women whose names had come up, and each admitted to spending some after-hours "quality time" with Ken on his couch.

We then confronted Ken, and he didn't deny it. In fact, he was more than a little impressed with himself and his exploits! (Proud enough to have started the rumors himself? I never found out.)

All parties were adults. All parties consented. The sofa sex took place after hours, so it wasn't interfering with work. But Ken was fired just the same, and not because he was canoodling on company property.

Rank Does Not Have These Privileges

Bad enough for any employee, from a janitor to a high-ranking executive, to carry on this way in the workplace. The office is not a motel, and if management looks the other way, the company is facing all kinds of risk.

But the big issue in this case was that Ken was the boss. The specter of a hostile work environment—the possibility that these women might have felt pressured into the liaison, or that playing the couch game might have been seen as the route to advancement—hangs heavy over these kinds of situations. Even if Ken never suggested that the women would get ahead by getting busy with him (or, more sinisterly, that there would be negative consequences for anyone who didn't play along), the women might have feared that would be the case or might have claimed as much later. Or, if one of them were promoted ahead of another employee, it might be claimed that the decision was based on sexual performance rather than job performance.

Whether or not there was actual pressure or duress from Ken as the boss, the appearance and the possibility are enough to create a problem for the company.

By the way, gender didn't factor in: we've dealt with similar situations where the genders were reversed, with the same outcome.

Now we know what happened to the people, but what about the (in)famous couch?

It, too, was "terminated." Despite being cleaned and disinfected, it was ultimately discarded. No one in the company wanted it, given its storied history.

TIPS

Dirty Dating

- If you're going to get involved with someone at work—and many people do, given that they spend so much time there—stick with people at your own level or in a different chain of command. Supervisor/supervisee sexual relations of any kind are a bad idea, even if you take it off-site. If you can't find anyone appropriate to sleep with, you really need to get out more.
- If you're the subordinate, you may think you have to accept a boss's advances to stay on his or her right side. You don't. Talk to HR if you feel at all pressured.

- Using a relationship with the boss to get ahead is just plain wrong. And do you really want to have a reputation as someone who sleeps his or her way to the top, or whose only skills are horizontal? That won't help your vertical movement in the organization when your boss moves on and you report to someone else.
- If you're the boss, it's just as wrong to use your power over subordinates to get into their pants. Even the illusion of that is a career killer. Part of your responsibility as a supervisor is being alert to how your power—even when it seems like you don't have much power at all—can be perceived.
- Even if none of that is true—nobody is pressuring anyone, nobody is looking to get anything out of the fling except a good time—the rest of the office will suspect otherwise. The damage to both your careers that office rumors can create can be just as severe.
- The office furniture is meant for business use. It doesn't matter how nice that couch is, it's not there for your pleasure.

MEMO TO MANAGEMENT

Executive perks may include a snazzy leather couch. But they do not entitle executives to seduce subordinates upon that couch . . . or anywhere else in the office, for that matter.

If an inappropriate employee relationship comes to light, address it. And make sure employees understand what is appropriate and what isn't.

In general, allowing a fast and loose office environment can result in accusations that upper management tolerated, or worse yet, encouraged inappropriate behavior. Be on the lookout for telltale signs of interpersonal problems at the office. Like the old saying, "Where there is smoke, there is fire," rumors of shenanigans at the office usually have at least some element of truth to them. Diligently follow smoke trails and you will most often find some fire.

CASE FILE
Presidential Privilege

Yet another male executive claimed to be very sensitive to stress and in need of periodic "relief" during the workday. He thought the appropriate solution was to solicit—and receive—oral sex from coworkers in his office. Once again, people started talking, and eventually the talk made it to Human Resources.

When we asked this executive about the rumors, it didn't take a congressional hearing to get him to admit what had been going on. He was shocked to hear he was being fired as a result. "If Bill Clinton could do it," the nonplussed (and soon-to-be-former) executive told me, "I thought I could, too."

TIPS
Executive Directive

- You are not Bill Clinton.
- President Clinton may not be the best role model when it comes to sexual behavior at the office. And if what allegedly

happened in the Oval Office—one of the most secure places in the world—leaked out, why would things be any different in your own office?

MEMO TO MANAGEMENT

A company should have formal HR training seminars at the office and make it mandatory that all employees attend and sign a statement confirming their attendance. These seminars should include sexual harassment and hostile workplace training issues. It is very helpful to create a paper trail of proactive measures like this in case trouble arises down the road. It is important and helpful for companies to portray and enforce a "zero tolerance" for the type of activity described in this book. Written policies and consistently implemented practices go a long way toward that goal.

Most employees, of course, are diligent and hard-working, deserving praise rather than punishment. At one company, we rewarded the top ten sales performers of each quarter with a party at a very expensive restaurant with unlimited food and drink. We assumed that our best employees—disciplined, dedicated workers, the cream of the crop—would be able to control themselves. And mostly we were right. Mostly.

At one of these events, Sally, a normally reserved salesperson, overdid it with the unlimited alcohol. Sally had a few, then a few more. First she grew flushed, then animated, then flirtatious.

Then it went from amusing to a slow-motion car wreck.

Sally tugged her top down to display her cleavage, telling her colleagues, "Have a look at my assets."

Then she pulled her top farther down, popped open her bra, and put those assets into plain view. But apparently flashing the team wasn't enough. "Come on, guys, pull my top down!" she invited. "Let me show you what I've got."

She wasn't the only one who'd been drinking. She wasn't the only one whose judgment was impaired. It's probably needless for me to say that she found takers.

Nobody was so drunk they didn't remember. The next day, the whole episode became an office joke, with Sally as its butt.

Afterward, Sally summoned the police and charged one of the colleagues who'd pulled her top down with assaulting her. She also filed a claim with the Equal Employment Opportunity Commission (EEOC), which we felt she'd done so that she couldn't be fired without the suspicion that the action had been in retaliation for filing charges.

Not the kind of drama any workplace needs. And not good for Sally's career. She went from being a sales superstar to falling apart because of the aftershocks from her behavior.

She quit two months later.

That was the last of these parties we hosted.

TIPS

Truth or Dare

- Yanking off a coworker's blouse or pants is probably not a wise move, even with an engraved invitation! What may start as consensual "fun" with a coworker can turn ugly fast. Keep your guard up at all times. When a person's job is in jeopardy, they may go to great lengths to save it, including hurling serious accusations.

- If you wouldn't do it sober in the office, don't do it drunk at a company-sponsored event. You may not be on-site or on the clock, but if the company is picking up the tab, you will probably pay for any bad behavior. Do you really want to be known as the office boob?

MEMO TO MANAGEMENT

Having alcohol at a company event, on or off premises, can lead to trouble. No matter how carefully you monitor such situations, there is always the potential for a messy, combustible outcome.

CASE FILE
Showing Himself a Little Love

Sex at the office doesn't have to be a two-way street! One high-level manager at one of the firms I worked at kept his office stocked with several bottles of liquor, a DVD player, and a library of pornographic videos. When he was bored or didn't feel like working, he closed his door, poured himself a drink, chose a movie from his extensive X-rated video collection, and, shall we say, entertained himself.

At least he closed the door before his private party. At least he had a door to close.

It is amazing how often employees are caught downloading and/or watching porn at the office, even in open work areas in plain view of everyone.

TIPS

Movie Hour

- It's one thing to take a break for a cup of coffee or a quick trip to the gym, but watching pornography at your desk is not an appropriate way to de-stress during office hours. Save movie hour for after hours.
- Streaming or downloading porn (or anything else, for that matter) is probably a violation of company policy . . . unless it's research for your job, but good luck proving that one to the HR department.
- If you can see someone else's computer, they can probably see yours. And report what they see. And remember what I said about the company watching your email? Same goes for the websites you visit and the files you download.

MEMO TO MANAGEMENT

Site-blocking software. Site-blocking software. Site-blocking software.

CASE FILE

Judging by Appearance

Jim thought he was being a gentleman when he told his colleague Liz, "I love the way that dress looks on you. Really beautiful."

A couple days later, they met in the elevator. "Good morning! You look great in that sweater today," he said. Liz muttered something in response, Jim thought nothing of it, and went on with his day. Until he was called into the HR manager's office.

Male employees are often the subject of complaints for making what they claim are innocent compliments to female coworkers. Jim certainly thought that's all he was doing. But from Liz's point of view, it looked different: she thought by focusing on her appearance, he was hitting on her. And that made her uncomfortable.

When I counsel male employees about things like this, I tell them that to be safe, any casual comments should not be based on the gender of the person to whom they are speaking. For example, would you say the same thing to a male colleague? If not, then don't say it to a female. Remember, we're all there for the same reason—to do a job—and the fact that you find someone or something attractive, while a perfectly normal thing to think, doesn't contribute to getting the job done. Everyone at the workplace wants to be valued for their work. If you're eager to compliment someone, pointing out a job well done or a problem solved is a better choice.

It's not just about gender, either. If you say something to a gay colleague, would you say the same thing to a straight colleague? (Or *about* such a colleague?) It's increasingly common for companies to have policies in place explicitly extending workplace protections to gay, lesbian, and transgender individuals. Everyone at the workplace is on the same team, no matter which team they're playing for.

What you might intend as an innocent remark may strike your fellow employee as contributing to a hostile work environment and lead to a complaint against you. That does not mean you can't say anything nice about anyone at any time! Just take a moment to reflect before opening your mouth. A little common sense will go a long way.

On the Flip Side

If you are on the receiving end of what you feel are inappropriate remarks or actions, or if you feel you are being unfairly treated by your company for any reason, follow your company's policies for reporting such treatment. (They're probably in that employee handbook you got when you were hired then stuck in the bottom of a drawer, never to be seen again. Now is the time to dig it out.) If there are no policies, you should let an uninvolved member of management know about your concerns. For example, first raise your concerns with the HR department or the general counsel of the company. If the company has neither, contact a high-ranking and uninvolved executive. Make sure to independently document all such communications. Note that this doesn't mean you should secretly record your conversations! (Depending where you are, that might open a different legal can of worms.) But it can be helpful, should matters escalate, to have notes available, especially because memory isn't 100 percent reliable. Only if all else fails should aggrieved employees consult with a trusted labor attorney to see if their rights have been violated and to explore potential remedies.

Filing a lawsuit should always be a measure of last resort. It is a difficult, drawn-out, and unpredictable process. Yes, it puts some pressure on the company to resolve the matter in order to avoid the time, hassle, expense, and publicity of litigation. But at the same time, your whole background becomes fair play—what websites you visit; what you've said to co-workers, friends, and family about the issue; what you do in your free time; prior disciplinary problems at other jobs—everything is fair game. Plus, recognize that future employers may not want to hire you if they find out that you have sued a prior employer—remember, lawsuits are a matter of public record. Even if you win your suit, all other qualifications being equal, an employer may be wary of someone who has a history of suing his or her employer. That might not be fair. But it is a possibility.

TIPS

Sweet Talk

- If you wouldn't want someone to say it to you, don't say it to someone else at work.
- If you wouldn't say it to a colleague of the same sex or sexual orientation, don't say it to someone of a different sex or sexual orientation.
- Even if you don't say something potentially offensive directly to someone, they're likely to hear it or hear about it. Keep it to yourself.
- Colleagues want to feel valued and respected for their contributions, just like you do. Does what you're about to say contribute to that? If so, great. If not, zip your lip.

MEMO TO MANAGEMENT

Make sure you have policies in place about what is appropriate and what is not in the workplace. The line between friendly conversation and remarks that marginalize employees or make them uncomfortable is not always easy for the average person to identify. Clear examples can help your employees understand the difference.

CASE FILE
Pay to Play

HR departments are often put in the uncomfortable position of concealing off-site affairs because they bubble over into the workplace. Not pretty.

Cash was a high-ranking business executive, married at the time, who invited a young female employee to join him on his private boat on a Friday afternoon. This was not a business trip, as you've probably guessed. They both drank too much, and on the way home from the boating excursion, the female employee was involved in a serious car accident. It was bad enough that the young woman was hurt because two employees were irresponsible and created a situation where she drank and drove.

Feeling guilty after the fact and worried that his actions might come back to haunt the company, Cash told me what had happened. He worried that his lady friend would spill the beans about where she'd been and (more importantly) with whom. Not good for his business—or his marriage. His solution: he offered the young lady $10,000 (of his own money, mind you, not the company's) to keep what happened "quiet."

It is common for companies to offer a severance package to certain employees when they quit or are let go. In exchange for money, exiting employees sign waivers and releases of all claims. It can be a win-win for the employee and company: The company gets some peace of mind, knowing that the employee can't sue them for anything after signing such an agreement, and the employee gets extra money on the way out the door.

But that's not what happened here. This wasn't about ending a business relationship with a no harm, no foul agreement. This was about saving Cash's bacon, or so it appeared. There was nothing illegal about it—he didn't ask her to lie to the police or not report a crime, or anything of that nature—but it's still dodgy, because shelling out money quickly sure makes a person look guilty, doesn't it?

Cash claimed he was just trying to help out with the medical expenses and car repairs and minimize general inconvenience, since it had happened in the aftermath of their outing. Asking her to keep her mouth shut in return was secondary, he claimed.

That is a risky thing for the company and executive. Even if everything Cash said were true, it would have been easy for the young lady to make things unpleasant. The fact that he whipped out his checkbook so quickly certainly points to him being responsible for the accident, and if she had chosen to sue, that's how judge or jury might see it. Moreover, because of their relationship—employer and employee—the company and its assets could easily have been dragged into the situation.

And you can bet if it had come to all that, Mrs. Cash would hear all about it.

TIPS

Money Talks

- If you are offered money as part of a severance agreement, have an attorney review the agreement before signing it. Take your time and do not rush into signing, no matter how tempting the money may seem.
- Don't let anyone make you feel pressured to sign on the spot. You're entitled to get legal advice and to sleep on it before signing.
- Employers may routinely offer money to resolve a matter in order to avoid disruption of business. The offer doesn't

necessarily mean the company thinks anybody has done anything wrong.

- If you are offered extra money without an agreement to sign, that may be a red flag. Look closely and ask questions, because something fishy may be going on.

MEMO TO MANAGEMENT

In today's highly litigious world, the smart company uses severance agreements to curtail the risk of legal claims by problematic or hostile employees. It is usually pretty easy to determine which employees are likely to be more volatile than others. Paying some extra consideration to secure a lock-solid severance agreement is a cheap form of insurance to avoid potentially costly and protracted legal battles. During my career, I have prepared and distributed more than 350 different severance agreements. Out of those 350 agreements, fewer than five employees refused to sign them. Of the 350 people to whom I presented severance agreements, not one ever sued or brought any type of claim. The moral of this story? Severance agreements work.

True Romance

Not every instance of office flirtation is inappropriate. Most of us spend more of our waking hours at our jobs than anywhere else, often working in close quarters with colleagues. It's no surprise, then, that a coworker may catch your eye and an actual office romance develop. There are lots of appealing aspects to dating a coworker: it's convenient, time efficient, and you can carpool.

Before embarking on such an adventure, however, check your company's policies. Some may prohibit two employees dating; others may only forbid fraternizing between lower-level employees and their supervisors. Some have no rules against it at all. Make sure you know whether your flirtation may be stepping over any lines.

TIPS

Mixing Business and Pleasure

A few tips if you do want to pursue a workplace romance:

- Look beyond the adjacent cubicle. Date outside your department or area. You may hope to be inseparable, but a little distance in the workplace can be a good thing, even if policy doesn't demand it.
- Have a plan if the romance goes south. Talk with your paramour about it. Remember, you're still going to have to work together, and if things get ugly between you, you don't want it getting ugly for the entire office. Trust me, that is not a good career move.
- Set boundaries. Discuss where the line between work and personal will be because if one of you thinks it's fine to chat with office friends about *every* personal thing and the other isn't comfortable with the guy in the next cube knowing what kind of underwear you prefer, that's going to be an issue. You might even conduct "trust tests" early on—revealing something innocuous about yourself to your love interest and then waiting to see if this information makes its way to other coworkers.
- As unromantic as it may sound, sometimes it's prudent to put the consensual nature of the relationship in writing. I'm

not saying you need a pre-nup just to ask out the person across the hall, but you do want to think about the potential consequences to your job. When a supervisor dates someone who works for him or her, it's all too easy for the lower-level employee to turn around later, when the bloom is off the rose, and claim he or she felt compelled to participate in the relationship, that his or her job was in jeopardy, that he or she couldn't say no.

Too often, office romances end badly on both a personal and professional level, and the consequences can go well beyond a simple broken heart. Prepare for the worst case and hope for the best.

CHAPTER 2

Inferior Superiors

Bosses from Hell

The quirks and foibles of superiors are usually seen as an unavoidable part of the job. Who hasn't had to deal with a "difficult" manager? Sometimes, however, behavior crosses the line from ill-mannered or eccentric to flat-out unbearable. Being publicly humiliated by an irate supervisor in front of colleagues or screamed at because you put half-and-half in someone's coffee instead of one-percent milk can be pretty demoralizing, especially when it happens on a regular basis. Often we just resign ourselves to enduring it while quietly seething at our desks.

But it doesn't have to be that way. What recourse do you have in the face of incompetent or abusive management?

Many executives and higher-ups are adept at keeping their inappropriate conduct confined to a gray area that defies outright classification as "harassment" or "hostile work environment," but sometimes it's easy to tell when actions cross the line.

CASE FILE
Showered with Attention

A senior executive was known for telling prospective employees that he "would make the best ruler this universe had ever seen." Let's just say he had no problems with self-esteem. This ruler-of-the-universe was also inordinately proud of his physique. To maintain that physique, he had a private office that boasted a weight room and shower.

He liked to show off that physique, especially to female employees. He would call them into his office for a "meeting." When they arrived, they found him clad in nothing but a towel, fresh from the shower after a workout. He conducted the whole meeting in the towel, as blithely unconcerned as the emperor in his new clothes.

More than one of his female staff objected to this display, calling it harassment when they gave their notice. As we discussed in Chapter 1, it's not unheard-of for a company to ask an employee to sign a release in return for compensation, and indeed, these offended female employees were paid a substantial amount of money to sign such a release on the way out the door.

You'd think that, after a couple of these payments, the company would wise up and get rid of Mr. Ruler-of-the-Universe or at least put a halt to his loincloth-clad meetings. Not necessarily.

Just about everything in business is about the balance sheet. Mr. Ruler-of-the-Universe not only pumped himself up; he pumped up the company's bottom line as a major "rainmaker" who was absolutely critical to the organization. Whatever the company paid out to distressed female staff was more than made up by the amount of money this erstwhile Tarzan brought in.

"I WAS THINKING OF INTRODUCING 'DRESS DOWN FRIDAYS' – WHAT DO YOU THINK, GIRLS?.."

Not unpredictably, once this pattern had been established by repetition—towel-clad meeting leads to employee getting paid not to make a stink—women reporting to Mr. Ruler-of-the-Universe started to think of it as an entitlement, a severance bonus they were owed for putting up with this behavior. And maybe they were owed, given that the company had decided to put up with it, too.

This fellow was, in essence, untouchable, like the business equivalent of a tenured college professor, because of the money he brought in. In such cases, short of an act of God or an outright criminal act, he would continue to get away with it without the stern written reprimand, followed by firing, a normal employee would face.

TIPS

How to Rule the Universe

- No matter how hard you've been working out, unless your job description includes modeling your six-pack abs, keep your clothes on at work. All of them.
- Even if you are a huge rainmaker for your company, management can change, or the payouts can catch up to the rain made. Don't assume you're untouchable. Sooner or later, you won't be.
- No matter how adept you are sure you would be at ruling the universe, it is best to keep this opinion to yourself.

MEMO TO MANAGEMENT

Wise management impresses upon all employees, including the most senior of executives, that there are limits to acceptable behavior. If an executive is so powerful that his or her out-of-control behavior cannot be checked, then you have given that executive the potential power to take down your whole organization.

And if you are the rainmaker, you had better make sure the people under you sign that release on the way out the door!

CASE FILE
The Culinary Perfectionist

It is not at all unusual for executives with huge egos and difficult personalities to pay their employees a lot of money to tolerate a lot of abuse. That abuse often takes the form of very particular demands and unique personal requirements.

One executive, Pete, had his lunch prepared for him each day with very specific requirements. You might guess that he was a gourmet, demanding only the finest cuisine, or a health nut, determined not to pollute his body with toxic ingredients, or even an allergy sufferer who had to avoid certain foods or ingredients. Any of those might make some kind of sense. But not so in Pete's case.

This executive demanded that exactly four Pringles brand potato chips—no more and no less—be placed on the dish with his meal. They must be completely intact and unbroken—partial or chipped chips didn't count or represented an unforgiveable error on the part of the poor, suffering minion tasked with supplying his lunch.

At least his executive assistant knew this. Pity the poor, suffering temp filling in for a vacationing staffer, who didn't get the potato chip memo and delivered lunch with (gasp!) the wrong kind and number of chips.

The yelling, screaming meltdown could be heard in every corner of the floor.

Nor was this Pete's only culinary eccentricity. I was in a conference room speaking with our office porter when Pete's assistant burst into the room and yelled to the porter, "Thank God I found you! I've been looking all over for you. Pete needs his bagel right away – get downstairs now!"

As I learned from the porter later, Pete was convinced that only this employee, in the entire company, knew the "right" way to toast and cut up his bagel. No other hands were permitted, under any circumstances, to touch it.

Divergence from Pete's very precise demands invariably led to a crazed reaction. *Irate* doesn't even begin to cover it. With these kinds of people, hostility and anger management issues will often creep into every aspect of their lives, and hence every aspect of work.

Pete's persnickety ways were evident as well in his interviewing style. No potential job candidate could meet his unachievable expectations. He would routinely belittle job candidates for what he called their "stupid" responses. After receiving several complaints from job applicants, whenever possible we kept Pete out of the recruitment process. However, when it came to hiring a new personal assistant for Pete (surprised there was a vacancy in that plum job?), there was no avoiding him. After all, the candidate would be working closely with him and might as well know what he or she was getting into.

Did I mention that, at this point, Pete was twice divorced? Shocking, I know.

During a first interview with a prospective assistant, an attractive woman, Pete told her, "I am not sure I will hire you for the position, but I'm pretty sure you will end up being my wife."

He did hire her, and in due course, he also married her. Not surprising from his point of view, used as he was to getting his way, but I'm not sure what she was thinking, especially after she'd worked with him.

They were divorced in less than two years. I guess she never figured out just how he liked his bagel. Pete must have had some appeal that wasn't obvious to the rest of us, though: he's been married twice more since then.

CASE FILE

Nobody's Perfect (Enough)

A high-level partner at a law firm was a fitness nut. That didn't just mean that he was obsessed with his own fitness: he was obsessed with everyone else's as well. He routinely told employees they were fat or complained that they had no business eating fattening foods. He was known to snatch a bag of chips or candy out of an employee's hands if he or she dared even possess such a thing in his presence. His obsession with appearance also extended to how staff dressed. He complained if he thought anyone in his office wore "cheap" clothes or outfits that he didn't approve of.

But even if a staff member looked and dressed perfectly, there was no pleasing this unpleaseable fellow. Anything that wasn't done to his precise specifications, which included reading his mind, was deemed "****ing everything up." Once, his assistant had trouble deciphering his notoriously bad handwriting in order to give him a phone number that he had written down but neglected to copy into his cell phone before leaving on a trip. He demanded to know if she was "****ing stupid" and called her an "idiot" for not having transcribed the number immediately and not having put it in his cell phone for him. Never mind that because he was the one who had taken down the number, the assistant never knew the number existed until he called her to find it.

This man made people so anxious that some employees literally had nosebleeds after dealing with him! But he was another high-powered, "untouchable" individual. If employees didn't like his comments, their only recourse was to quit. Because the firm paid top dollar (probably because that's what it took to get people to come work there; reputations tend to spread quickly within an industry), people stayed and collected their hazardous-duty pay until they reached the absolute breaking point. Only then did they jump ship.

Executives of this stripe can burn through dozens or even hundreds of assistants. Many remain shockingly obtuse. Instead of wondering why all their assistants quit, they ask, "Isn't there at least one decent assistant in this city?"

I heard of one boss, also an attorney, whose assistants sometimes didn't last through the first day. More than one waited for the boss to go to lunch, left a note on his desk, resigning, grabbed their coats, and left. When he found one he liked, he delivered his highest compliment: "You're less stupid than most of the others."

One female executive with a big ego was having problems retaining an assistant. She was an abusive and totally demanding individual who had gone through more than *eighty* assistants—all female—in nine years. I thought she *might* be slightly less abusive to a man, so I suggested she try hiring a male assistant. By that time, anything was worth a try.

In response to my suggestion, the woman replied, "No, I've tried that before. The trouble is that every male assistant I hire ends up getting a crush on me." I think she was mistaking fear for love.

TIPS

One Easy Tip for Keeping an Assistant

Treat your assistant like you would want to be treated. News flash: Calling people names doesn't engender trust or loyalty. And is it really a productive use of your time to have to train a new person every week?

TIPS

If Your Boss Is the Asshole

You're not obligated to put up with abuse.

- Decide how much it's worth to you, personally and professionally, to keep this job. If you can let it roll off you and collect the paycheck, great. Bullies get their satisfaction from making people cower. If you don't cower, the bully *may* lose interest.
- Talk to Human Resources. If it's the first time, they will want to know. They can't fix it if they don't know about it.
- If your boss goes through staff like tissues during allergy season, HR already knows that it's the boss, not you, that's the problem. Management will have to determine how much the boss is worth to the company, and if he or she is worth a lot, HR may not be able to solve the problem. But it's worth a try because not all abusive bosses are as untouchable as they think they are.

MEMO TO MANAGEMENT

An executive with anger-management or other issues relating to interpersonal relationships may not be satisfied with treating employees badly. Such behavior has a tendency to spill over into external business relationships as well. Once a higher-up realizes that he or she can behave in any fashion with impunity, unprofessional behavior has a tendency to escalate. Reflect carefully on whether that is consistent with smart business practices and what the consequences will be to your company if this executive starts treating business partners with the same arrogance he or she shows to staff. This could be a disaster in the making for your company. Nip it in the bud if you can.

CASE FILE

You Can Sleep when You're Dead—If this Job Doesn't Kill You First

Sometimes, assistants are forced to mistreat other employees on behalf of their bosses. With their own jobs at stake, loyalty to peers can go out the window. One managing partner was a night owl. As a result, so was his assistant—whether she liked it or not. She never got lonely working those long nights: it was common for the night owl to order her to call employees at home about whatever he was working on—never mind that it might be three o'clock in the morning. No answering the call then rolling over and going back to sleep, either. "Get up, splash cold water on your face, and get into the office now!" the assistant ordered, at the night owl's behest. As a result, she was every bit as unpopular as he was.

"OF COURSE I DON'T MIND DRAGGING MYSELF OUT OF BED TO COME TO WORK AT THIS UNGODLY HOUR – I DO SOME OF MY BEST THINKING AT 1:45 AM!!"

Even the weekend is not sacred to some higher-ups. Another high-level executive, Wally, routinely scheduled meetings on weekends, just like it was another workday. He especially liked to schedule hour-long individual meetings with various teams of employees, starting at 11:00 a.m. on Saturday. Adding insult to injury—or perhaps injury to insult—Wally himself never bothered to arrive at the office until 2:00 p.m. or later, which threw the schedule wildly out of whack. His luckless subordinates didn't dare to show up late themselves, however, because Wally demanded that everyone be there at their assigned times, whether or not he was present—and he'd been known to check up on people. So the meetings might not actually start until 3:00 or 4:00 p.m. and would run until 9:00 or 10:00 p.m. on Saturday night.

Normally, if you are an hourly employee, you would be paid overtime to work extra hours like this. If you are a salaried employee ("exempt," in HR parlance), however, there are no time clocks and no overtime: you are expected to get the job done no matter what it takes. Most companies don't abuse that and may even let salaried employees slip out early occasionally in recompense for the times they work nights or weekends, but very long hours are not uncommon in certain industries and at certain companies. At Wally's place, it was take it or leave it. Everyone knew it was "the cost of poker," or what you did if you wanted to make the big bucks. You sucked it up, waited around for Wally to make his grand entrance, or risked losing your high-paying job.

So much for weekend plans.

CASE FILE
Weekend Warriors

In companies where staff are expected to work long hours, where everyone wants the boss to see them as the first one in the office and the last one out, some employees become experts in the fine art of office staging: making it look as though they are in the office early in the morning, late at night, or through the weekend without actually being there all the time. This involves such strategies as leaving office lights on; tossing a jacket over the back of the chair; scattering eyeglasses, half-consumed food, and open cans of soda on the desk (expert office stagers will warn against using coffee for this ruse; the boss can tell you're not there if it's been sitting there long enough to be ice-cold); and making sure the computer screen is on, with a document open. The idea is to make it look like you just stepped away for a minute (or the rapture came and snatched you up) should the boss happen by to check on your whereabouts when you have the audacity to go home.

Sometimes, setting such a clever scene isn't enough, especially in this electronic age. One minion, Terry, was assigned the unenviable task of monitoring whether or not employees came in on the weekend, and when and for how long, and reporting to a senior partner. Terry didn't want to have to spend the entire weekend circling the office checking who was really in and when. So she put technology to use for her.

On weekends, because the building's front desk wasn't staffed (to assure that only authorized personnel had access to the upper floors), one had to enter a passcode into a keypad to access the elevator bank. Each employee had a passcode, and building management could see exactly who had used the elevator and when during the off hours. Terry arranged to get a report from building security on Monday mornings, which she proudly presented to her boss as evidence who had come in when over the weekend. If an employee's name wasn't on Terry's list, he or she better have a darn good excuse—a medical emergency at the very least!

One poor soul had the temerity to tell Terry that he hadn't come in on the past weekend because he was caught up on all his work. He found himself with three new projects on his plate and quickly learned his lesson.

To encourage people to stay late and actually work, rather than just continuing to find ways to fake being at the office, one company ordered in and provided dinner for its employees every night at half past eight. Attendance at the communal dinner hour was highly encouraged—as in, if you want to be promoted, be at dinner. Everyone knows there is no such thing as a free lunch. That firm proved that there is no such thing as a free dinner, either!

TIPS

Getting a Life

- Leaving a spreadsheet or half-written email open on your computer may seem like a fail-safe way to look like you're still there hours after you make your exit, but technology has got you beat: your company may be monitoring exactly what you do on your computer and know that nary a keystroke has been made since four o'clock.
- If you're in one of those places where everyone competes to be the last one to leave, and you're staying late to win that contest, you might as well do actual work during that time. After all, if you care about this job enough to give up your evening or weekend for it, you might as well put in the effort

that will get you rewarded for those long hours with a raise or promotion.

- Nobody but you can decide how much you're willing to give up for your job. If you're trying to make an impression or are in a highly competitive field, long hours may be the price you pay for the chance to get ahead. If the demands become unreasonable or even unhealthy, you might point out to your boss that after a certain point, people are too tired to do quality work, and productivity suffers when things have to be redone.
- If your boss isn't hearing any of that, you might want to have a confidential conversation with your human resources representative. He or she may not know how hard people are being driven or may be able to give you a reality check about the situation. It may be that they can help you, or maybe you'll find that this just isn't the job for you.
- Depending what field you're in, or where you are, there may be rules limiting how many hours you can be employed to work. It's worth investigating if you think there's a problem.

MEMO TO MANAGEMENT

If you're in a position of power at your job, remember that you're an integral part of setting the tone at the office. Your behavior can determine whether people come to work filled with dread or with enthusiasm—and that will color not just their relationship with you but the quality of their work. Keeping people in the office until midnight just because you can, or losing your temper on an intern who's brought you the wrong sandwich, or watching over people's shoulders to make sure they are working every single minute—none of this flexing of your executive muscles will earn you respect or loyalty.

And what goes around comes around: an employee who is a mere minion today may at some point down the road—whether a year from now or a decade later—be a person from whom you need a favor. Or worse: he or she may end up as *your* boss!

CASE FILE
Talkative Tim

Tim was a manager who liked to catch people by phone—and once hooked, he didn't let anyone go. Once you picked up a call from Tim, you could plan on being chained to the phone for at least an hour, usually more. Not that you would be saying much: what Tim wanted, mostly, was an audience. He did all the talking. He seldom even stopped for a breath—a miracle of lung capacity.

Heaven forbid an underling tried to cut Tim short with a "Got to go now" or "I have another call" or "I'm really busy." Job number one, in Tim's view, was listening to him, and anyone who tried to cut him short was treated to an extra-long chewing-out.

One day, I was called down to the office of a senior executive—yes, even senior management fell prey to talkative Tim. When I got to the executive's office, he was on a phone call with Tim. Seeing me in his doorway, the executive signaled for me to come in and sit on the couch while he wrapped up his call with Tim. After five minutes or so with no sign of the conversation concluding (on this end it was mainly "uh huh" and similar sounds of acknowledgment), the executive finally put the phone receiver upside down in his lap and proceeded to have a fifteen-minute talk with me. The drone of Tim's monologue issuing from between the executive's thighs served as background to our conversation.

When we had finished our business, the executive lifted the receiver back to his ear. Tim hadn't even paused.

Suddenly the executive cut Tim off midstream, shouting: "Tim, *stop, stop. STOP*. You have been in my crotch for the last fifteen minutes, and if you don't shut up and listen to *me*, you are going right back to my crotch!"

This had the desired effect . . . at least until Tim's next phone call to an underling.

TIPS

The Forever Call

- Hygienically speaking, your crotch might not be the best place to put the phone—after all, it's going back up to your face later. A speaker phone with a mute button is a better solution for dealing with a long-winded caller and won't lead to someone walking into your office and wondering exactly what you're doing with that phone.
- Are *you* the endless interlocutor of your office? How long are your calls? Have you noticed people don't pick up if they know it's you? Make sure phone calls have a purpose and are concise and to the point. You don't want to end up in someone else's crotch, do you?

CHAPTER 3

Welcome to the Nut House

Your colleagues are your potential allies, the people in the trenches with you every day. When you want to commiserate about your heavy workload or gossip at the water cooler or just complain to someone about the new brand of coffee in the break room, these are your comrades. You probably spend more waking hours with your coworkers than you do with your family. And just like your family, some days you love them; other days, not so much. Just remember, if you tick them off (or they tick you off), you're still going to be stuck with them, so it's important to tread carefully.

In a perfect world, you'll love your colleagues more than you hate them, you'll have fun together at work, and each of you will look out for the other. If you *do* live in that perfect world, the rest of us envy you. But the rest of us, over the course of a career, meet and work with quite a mixture of characters. The key is learning how to get along with all of them.

"ON THE PLUS SIDE, SIR, WE'VE FINALLY SETTLED OUR DISAGREEMENT OVER THE DIRTY COFFEE FILTERS IN THE KITCHEN!"

CASE FILE

And in This Corner Office . . .

Two senior-level male employees were known to "butt heads" with each other frequently. Think of *The Odd Couple*: two more opposite sets of opinions—on every single thing—you'd be hard pressed to find. But unlike that odd couple, these two fellows did have a couple things in common: both had been athletes in school and both had very high opinions of themselves. Let the games begin!

Nobody remembered after the fact what this particular disagreement had been about—especially because disagreeing was standard operating procedure for these two tough guys. At any rate, the argument followed them out of a meeting and into the hallway. Voices were raised so that no one could miss it—and it being the hallway, they were right in the way of anyone who needed to get anywhere. That guaranteed them an audience.

One of the two men, a former star college football player whom we will call Larry, called the other a name. The other guy, Mikey, excelled in wrestling as a student. Mikey took exception to Larry's remark, poking a finger in Larry's chest. Larry answered with a shove. It didn't take much after that for the argument to escalate into a full-fledged fight.

And you can bet that before long, the entire office was assembled to watch.

Mikey had Larry in a headlock at one point, but Larry bulldozed his way free. The fight spilled up and down the hall, bouncing off the walls, with startled coworkers dodging out of the way. Finally, Larry hauled off and slammed Mikey into—and right through—the drywall. That was enough to end the fight.

No word on whether there was an office pool on the outcome.

TIPS

The First Rule of Office Fight Club

Don't start a fight in the office. That's the first rule. That's the only rule, really. But in case you need more . . .

- An office fistfight might be entertaining, but assault is a crime. Keep your emotions in check and your hands to yourself. Act like an adult, even if you don't feel like it.
- It doesn't matter who starts it; if you engage in a fight in the office, you're probably both going to get fired. Hotheads represent a risk to the company. Remember when they told you in grade school that it didn't matter who started it? That was a good lesson.
- If a coworker does start a fight with you, walk away and alert management. The good thing about being in an office is that you probably have witnesses.
- If you feel threatened by someone—someone who hasn't gotten physical, but is aggressive enough that it might be a concern—bring the situation to the attention of HR. Unless you work for the WWF, they have a strong interest in keeping things from escalating.

MEMO TO MANAGEMENT

Aggressive, competitive employees can be a good thing—but not if unchecked emotions get out of hand. Keep an eye on episodes of verbal aggression so you can address the situation before it devolves into physical aggression. Broken walls and furniture are costly, and broken bones are a big liability risk.

CASE FILE
Booger Down

We all have bad habits. Some habits are more annoying to coworkers than others. One employee, Karen, had a bad habit that, although it didn't affect her work performance, definitely had an impact on her relationships with colleagues. When she was talking to others, apparently without being conscious of it, her hands made their way to her nose—and inside for a little prospecting. As you can imagine, colleagues often opted to communicate with her in email rather than witness another expedition into Snotland. But sometimes the nature of the job necessitated a face-to-face conversation. But nobody wanted to be the one to face her down over her bad habit.

Finally, a coworker took it upon herself to type an anonymous message and leave it on Karen's desk: "Karen, we all have our annoying little habits. Sometimes, we don't know we have them unless others tell us. We want you to be aware that you have an unpleasant habit of constantly picking your nose." You can only imagine how embarrassing it would be to receive a note like that. But it worked . . . for about four months. After that, habit won out, and Karen went right back to picking her nose.

Ingrained habits are hard to break.

CASE FILE
Making a Stink

Many companies have dress codes, but fewer have formal written policies on personal hygiene. Perhaps more of them should.

Rodney must not have been paying attention when the rest of us learned as children about bathing, brushing our teeth, using deodorant, and so forth. Or maybe, to give him the benefit of the doubt, a colleague suggested he was showering before going to the gym and not after. Or perhaps this was his strategy to avoid having to share an office with anyone and assure his privacy at work. Whatever the case, it wasn't Rodney's reputation that preceded him; it was his aroma.

If something like that happens once or twice, it's natural to assume there are extenuating circumstances—the hot water wasn't working at his place; he spent the night somewhere other than home; he's having a particularly stressful day. But in Rodney's case, the scent was part of the package. Nobody wanted to sit next to him in meetings. The elevator would come, the doors would open, and Rodney would be the only one on board as everyone else decided they had suddenly forgotten something and would catch the next one.

Fortunately, Rodney wasn't in a public-contact role. Bad enough that our employees had to smell his odor, but imagine the consequences to business if he had been stinking customers out of the place.

Nevertheless, it was a problem. At first, a colleague with whom he was on friendly terms agreed on behalf of his peers to talk to Rodney.

The next day, he showed up doused in drug-store cologne. It was a different aroma, but just as strong and just as unpleasant to work around. Rodney's colleagues brought the matter to Human Resources. I drew the short straw and had to talk to Rodney about his personal hygiene.

Rodney claimed he'd read an article somewhere that said showering daily wasn't good for the skin. He remembered his grandfather talking about the "Sunday night bath" tradition of Grandpa's youth on a farm. Rodney had decided that if bathing once a week had been good enough for Grandpa, it was good enough for him.

I explained to Rodney that what might have made sense on a farm a few generations ago did not do for an office today. While I wasn't going to insist that he shower every single day, I noted that if anyone else could tell he hadn't showered, that was a sign that he was not showering frequently enough. We also discussed the value of such modern conveniences as underarm deodorant. I pointed out that it would not only be good for his career to bathe more frequently, but it might benefit his personal life as well.

"No, my girlfriend is fine with me the way I am," he told me.

I guess he was dating a farmer.

TIPS

Scent Sense

Rodney had a rationale behind his personal habits, but more than once I've had to speak with an employee about hygiene and learned that the employee was completely unaware of the issue and had never been taught what most of us consider customary cleanliness. Just in case you are one of those who missed out, here is what you need to know:

- Bathe regularly. Most Americans shower daily, but if you don't dig ditches for a living or do anything physically strenuous, you can probably skip a day here and there. To be clear: if anyone can see dirt on you or smell you, you are not bathing frequently enough.
- Deodorant/antiperspirant products are valuable, especially for men. I know there has been some controversy about certain ingredients in these products, but there are natural brands on the market if you prefer to avoid certain chemicals.

- Wash your hair regularly. Nothing says "ick" like greasy, stringy hair.
- If you have dandruff, use a dandruff shampoo; there are different products on the market for different types of dandruff, and if those don't work for you, your doctor can prescribe clinical-strength versions. No matter how clean you are, a snowfall on your shoulders looks unpleasant and puts people off.
- Brush your teeth in the morning and evening. Use toothpaste. (Yes, I have had to tell someone that part.) For bonus points with your dentist and coworkers, brush after every meal. Some employees keep a travel-size toothbrush and toothpaste in a desk drawer in case they need to freshen up. Just don't spit toothpaste all over the bathroom sink.
- Mouthwash and mints are good to keep around for fending off coffee breath or if you've had a particularly fragrant lunch.
- Clothes can smell, too. Make sure the clothes you wear to work are clean. If you're a smoker or a pet owner, even freshly laundered items can pick up odors from your morning cigarette or playing with your big, wet dog. Fabric-freshening products such as Febreze are helpful in those cases. Those products also remove the stale smell from clothes that may have been in storage during the summer or winter months.
- Be stingy with scented products. Heavy perfumes can be just as offensive to the nose as body odor or bad breath. Moreover, some people experience severe allergies to perfumes, either on their own or in hair and body products. Use scented products sparingly. Good scent or bad, no one should smell you coming.

MEMO TO MANAGEMENT

Nothing in my legal and professional training prepared me for these kinds of personal conversations with employees. When you are in the position to have one, it will be uncomfortable. Remember that the situation is even more uncomfortable for the person you're having the conversation with.

Keep things professional and fact-based. Keep names of employees who have complained out of it. This is a business issue: the employee is making others uncomfortable and not presenting himself or the company in a good light. Maintain a positive approach. You are having the conversation to help this person resolve the issue so it doesn't get in the way of your company's business or his or her career.

If the employee is from another country, be sensitive to the fact that there may be cultural differences in play. Scented American shampoos are considered unpleasant in certain parts of the world. Foods that are common elsewhere may not be noticed on someone's breath in that country, but may seem strong and offensive here. If culture is an issue, enlighten the employee to the customs in your region and in your industry.

You may want to schedule a follow-up meeting with the employee to make sure all is going well on the personal hygiene front. That will keep both you and the employee from considering the matter concluded once the awkward talk is over and forgetting about it.

If you treat this like any other professional development issue, both you and the employee will be at least a little less uncomfortable, and you are more likely to have a good result.

"I THOUGHT IT WOULD BE BETTER TO TAKE ALL MY CIGARETTE BREAKS IN ONE GO!"

CASE FILE
Day Gone Up in Smoke

Cigarette smoking is one of the hardest habits to break, as any smoker, present or former, will attest. Some companies may be reluctant to hire smokers, as they worry that they may take more sick time because of smoking-related illness, or more breaks to take a smoke, now that the days of smoking in the office are long gone.

Joe was one of those. His job in customer service only permitted limited breaks, but he was always asking his coworkers to cover for him so he could sneak out for a smoke between scheduled breaks. These smoke breaks could get lengthy: in cold or wet weather, it meant getting into outerwear, then out of it when he returned, in addition to the smoking time; in any season, he might meet other smokers out on the sidewalk and extend his break to a second or third cigarette in order to finish a conversation.

Joe's nonsmoking colleagues liked the guy and didn't want to rat him out, but they felt taken advantage of. Nobody wanted to be the one to say anything, so they took to hiding his cigarettes. Unfortunately, that backfired, as his breaks now included running down the block to buy a new pack of smokes, in addition to the smoking time.

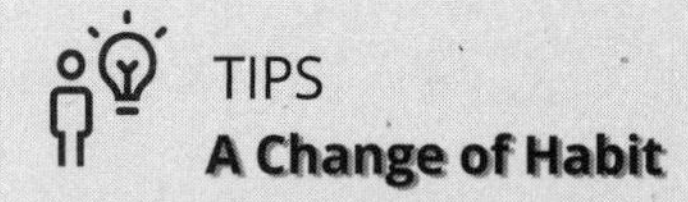

TIPS
A Change of Habit

How to get the message across to a coworker whose bad habits are affecting you:

- Be direct. Hinting around is easily overlooked or ignored (out of embarrassment), and passive-aggressive games like hiding the cigarettes don't solve the problem. Either determine to face up to the issue or learn to live with it.
- There's safety in numbers. If the bad habit or behavior is bothering you, it's probably bothering others. If you stand together, it's harder for the offender to believe that you're just fussy or touchy, and it's not really a problem for anyone else.
- Be honest but kind. The note to Karen was a good example: the sender acknowledged that Karen might not even realize what she was doing, but was clear about the fact that it bothered others.
- Make it about the issue, not the person. You're not saying the offender is a bad person (maybe he or she is, but that's a different problem); you're saying that the habit or behavior is the problem. Focus on *why* it's an issue for you: Karen's nose-picking is unpleasant to watch; Joe's smoke breaks are making you pull extra weight while he's out, or putting you in an awkward position covering for him with the boss.
- Remember, too, that you're not telling others how to run their lives (much as you may want to); if Joe wants to smoke, that's his business. Your business is whether his smoking affects you and your work.
- Put yourself in the other person's shoes. If you were the person who drums incessantly with a pen until the person at the next desk wants to leap over the cubicle wall and break the pen (or your hand), how would you want to receive the message that you're driving people around you crazy?

MEMO TO MANAGEMENT

Managers are often in a better position to solve these kinds of bad-habit problems by simply instructing the employee that it's not appropriate behavior. If, as a manager, you notice or are alerted to bad habits that bother others, a gentle but firm conversation can put the matter to rest.

Minor annoyances may seem petty, but if they are genuinely disturbing a group of workers, they are likely to be affecting efficiency or productivity. It may seem like a small matter and a waste of your valuable time, but if it's bothering a number of people, a quick conversation to solve it may be time well spent.

Other people's habits aren't necessarily anyone's business, especially if they don't affect the work. But that doesn't keep employees from anointing themselves the saviors of their coworkers.

One department had a tradition of celebrating birthdays with cake in the office. Kathleen was new to the department and thought this was a delightful tradition. Imagine her surprise when, after the candles were blown out and a colleague was cutting and handing out slices of cake, she was passed over. "You don't need any cake," her colleague said, pointing to Kathleen's girth. "I didn't want you to be tempted."

TIPS
None of Your Beeswax

Kathleen's colleague probably thought she was being helpful, assuming Kathleen was trying to lose weight. But unless a colleague specifically asks you for help with a personal issue or habit, you're best off not assuming and not stepping in. Adults can make their own decisions about their behavior. Making decisions for them is intrusive and rude.

CASE FILE
U Can't Touch These

A female employee whom we'll call Bobbie took vacation time for what she told close friends was a "silicon sabbatical," returning to the office with noticeably enhanced breasts. Some of her male colleagues took notice, often in inappropriate ways, calling attention to and making jokes about her new attributes. She brought a complaint about their behavior to Human Resources.

In the course of investigating, however, we learned that Bobbie had been messaging her female coworkers with complaints that the guys in the office weren't hot enough. "We need to hire some male eye candy around here, instead of these losers," she wrote.

Bobbie's bad behavior didn't make the men's remarks acceptable; nor did their bad behavior excuse Bobbie's remarks. Pretty much everyone behaved badly in this situation, and they all got to hear that message loud and clear from HR.

CASE FILE
Cleaning Up

Clare hated her job. She became friendly with a co-worker and regularly messaged her friend about how much she thought her job sucked. That might seem familiar—we all commiserate with colleagues when we're unhappy at work. Who better to understand your pain than someone who feels the same pain?

But Clare was motivated and resourceful and applied those qualities to looking for a way out of the job, one where she could actually clean up, as it so happened.

One day, she shared her master plan in a message to her friend: the two of them would quit their current jobs and start a house-cleaning service, specializing in cleaning rich people's homes.

Sounds like a good plan, right?

Unfortunately, Clare's detailed business plan included not just cleaning up, but cleaning out wealthy clients' homes. She had a step-by-step blueprint for how they could steal from the rich—and keep for themselves. She was sure they wouldn't get caught.

Clare never got the chance to test her mettle as a cleaning lady/criminal mastermind. Remember what we said in Chapter 1 about in-office communication not being private? In this case, Clare's friend helped the process, not by ratting her out to the bosses but by telling other colleagues about Clare's crazy plan. It wasn't long before Clare's dirty little secret made its way to management, who let her know exactly what they had learned. She was let go; we knew the authorities wouldn't prosecute her because she hadn't acted on her plans, but she didn't need to know that. Her future as a criminal mastermind was halted before it even got started.

TIPS

Thought Crimes

It's not against the law to think criminal thoughts (except in certain dystopian science fiction books and movies). Conspiracy to commit a crime may be actionable, but there are very specific requirements before anyone is likely to be charged with conspiracy. Clare's case was no more than talk, so it wasn't even brought to the authorities.

But companies are not limited to the law when finding grounds to discipline or dismiss an employee. Firing her was an open-and-shut case.

CASE FILE

Don't Look a Gift Horse in the . . .

It's not uncommon for employees to circulate a birthday card for a boss or colleague that everyone signs. It's a nice little thing that coworkers do for each other. Most of the time.

Art bought a card for his (female) boss for her birthday and passed it around the office for everyone to sign. He asked colleagues to return it to him after everyone had the chance to sign it. Everyone assumed he wanted to be the one to give it to the boss, so he'd get the brownie points: fair enough, since he'd sprung for the card and circulated it. But in fact, Art wanted to add his own artistic touch to the card before delivering it.

Art added a drawing in the card. A drawing of himself. A drawing of himself, completely nude with Arnold Schwarzenegger-like muscles, sitting on top of a gigantic birthday cake, a flatteringly sized candle strategically placed to leave little to the imagination.

Although he kept his clothes on at work, everyone knew Art had a near body-builder physique he was very proud of.

No one knew what he had done—but all their signatures were on the offending card. Art's colleagues were baffled when they were called into the conference room for a dressing-down from the boss about the dressed-down-to-nothing picture. It didn't take long for the truth of the circumstances to come out; in fact, Art was pretty proud of himself—and I don't just mean his artwork!

TIPS

Trust but Verify

Most of the time, when an employee takes the lead in doing something nice for someone else, it's out of genuine kindness and affection. Sometimes, it's to make him- or herself look good, whether to the boss, colleagues, or others. Most of the time, you can assume the best of a coworker. That's a route to good relationships in the workplace.

It's when someone changes hats that you might want to look more closely; when the always selfish person is suddenly generous, it *may* be that he or she had a visit in the night from three spirits and turned over a new leaf. But don't bet on it.

CASE FILE
Show Me the Money

Ron, who worked in accounting, was a busy guy, always on the run from one meeting or deadline to another, often with a pile of folders or sheaf of documents tucked under his arm. It was probably inevitable that he would eventually leave something somewhere. In fact, it probably happened more than once—but it was one particular time that caused a big stir.

It was annual budget time, so among the documents Ron was rushing around with were assorted departmental and corporate budgets—including one that listed each employee and his or her salary. Ron stopped off in the men's room between meetings, and when he rushed off to his next meeting, he left the salary document behind, next to the sink.

Only after an hour did he realize his mistake and retrace his steps, looking for the missing papers. By that time, of course, someone else had found the document—and juicy information like that spreads through a company with an efficiency that management can only wish for when there's work to be done. We never did find out who picked it up, but like the old commercial, he told two friends, and they told two friends, and so on, until most of the office knew everyone else's salary.

Now, there are a few companies that espouse radical transparency and make the salaries of everyone, top to bottom, available to everyone in the company. Those companies are rare, and this wasn't one of them.

Needless to say, there were a number of questions asked of supervisors about salaries—"How come Joe is getting more than I am, when we do the same job?"—and requests for raises—"I'm much more experienced than Sal over there, so I should make more." The culprit who spread the information was never identified, but Ron was reprimanded for being careless with confidential information.

At another company, a female vice president inadvertently received the salary figures for another department instead of her department, which revealed that her male counterpart in that department was being paid almost double what she was. When she confronted the president of the company about this, he shrugged and said, "I guess he negotiated better." She left shortly thereafter for a position elsewhere that paid three times what she had been making.

TIPS

I'll Show You Mine If You'll Show Me Yours

- Knowing what the going rate is for your job puts you in a much better position when you are negotiating salary. But getting that information by illicit means won't win you any points. Stick to internet research for that information.
- You may ask a peer to reveal his or her salary if you'll tell him or her yours. Be careful, though; some companies may have policies against sharing that information among coworkers. Also, think first about how it will affect your working relationship if you find that one of you is making significantly more than the other.
- If confidential salary information comes into your hands, think twice before sharing. Although we never discovered who circulated the information Ron left in the men's room,

if we had, that person would have been subject to disciplinary action; while Ron made a careless mistake, that person knew full well what he was doing was wrong.

- If you do find out someone else makes more than you do, or more than you think he or she is worth, you might think back to the story in the Bible about the vineyard workers who were hired later in the day and got the same pay as the workers who had been hired in the morning. When the workers who'd been there longer complained, the vineyard owner pointed out that he'd paid them what they'd agreed to when he hired them. The moral for the workplace is that what the other person gets paid isn't any of your business; your business is what you get paid. If you want to make a case for a raise, base it on the value you bring, not what someone else gets paid.

MEMO TO MANAGEMENT

Salary information is best held in confidence in most cases, but that doesn't mean it won't slip out. Your best defense, should that happen, is fair and equitable treatment of employees and even-handed, evidence-based performance evaluations.

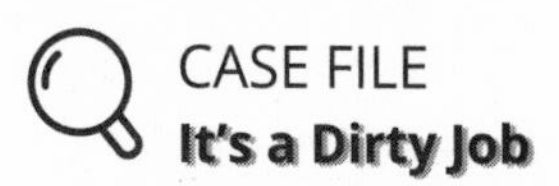

An executive called Chuck liked the ladies. Lots of ladies. Lots of ladies who were not his (presumably oblivious) wife. He was smart enough not to carry on with coworkers, but one woman in the office knew all about his extracurricular activities: his assistant, Ann, who was frequently tasked with sending flowers to Chuck's latest conquest, buying gifts for girlfriends—including lingerie. Chuck told her, "You've worked with me a long time. You know what I like. And you're a woman, so you'll know what she'll like. It's better if you pick something out." And indeed, Chuck's long-suffering assistant did know Chuck's taste, and he was always pleased with what she chose. (She never found out if Chuck's lady friends were as pleased. But since Chuck continued to send her shopping, she assumed they were.)

It was awkward enough that Ann was shopping for Chuck's conquests so frequently that she knew the sales staff at the high-end lingerie shop by their first names. But the breaking point came when Chuck announced on Friday at noon that he was leaving early for the day, and he needed Ann to pick up condoms for him when she went out for lunch.

Ann brought the request, and her discomfort with it, to the attention of the HR department. An HR representative had a little chat with Chuck about what was and wasn't an appropriate use of business resources—and employees count as business resources.

The next lady Chuck sent flowers to was Ann. And he placed the order himself.

TIPS

Not My Job, Man

Unless these things are explicitly in your job description or part of the nature of your work, you shouldn't feel you have to:

- Buy condoms, sex toys, or other highly personal items for a boss or coworker.

- Babysit for the boss's children, do their homework for them, or write their school papers or college application essays.
- Provide an alibi for the boss's indiscretions or get mixed up in a boss's personal relationships in any way.
- Provide computer support for the boss's family members or lend out company software for someone's personal use.
- Lie, cheat, or steal on your boss's behalf. (Leaving aside the kind of minor misdirections that are part of anyone's work life, like, "I don't want to talk to him. Tell him I just left.")

And yes, all of these are things I personally know that real employees have been instructed to do.

MEMO TO MANAGEMENT

It's common for executive assistants to provide a certain amount of personal support for top executives in order to free them to focus all their time on business needs. Still, there's a difference between picking up dry cleaning and buying condoms. Keeping good administrative support staff means keeping their responsibilities within the bounds of business propriety.

CASE FILE
It's There in Black-and-White

Manager Ty was a technophobe. He had risen in his career before the computer age, when secretaries were the only ones who knew how to use anything with a keyboard, and he had a hard time joining the modern era. The IT department had set up his computer to turn itself on at nine every morning and open the applications he would most likely need. But that wasn't enough; he watched key business information in one of the windows like he would sit in front of the TV, but never touched a single key himself.

Fortunately, Ty had a long-time assistant who handled all his communication, just as she had in the old days. She printed out his email for him to read on paper; he then dictated replies, which she emailed back under his name. Not the most efficient way to work, but it worked well enough for Ty.

That was true until a friend of Ty's discovered one of the most popular things on the internet—and I don't mean pictures of cats. Ty's buddy started emailing him pornographic photos that he found online.

Ty's assistant, Polly, was shocked, to say the least. At first, she assumed it was a mistake, or spam, and deleted the emails. But they kept showing up—and showing all.

Meanwhile, Ty's buddy was surprised that Ty wasn't showing any appreciation for his efforts in finding and sending the best of internet porn. They ran into each other and the friend asked Ty, obliquely because both their wives were present, why he hadn't replied to the emails he'd sent.

The next day, Ty called Polly into his office and gave her a firm dressing-down for not passing on *all* of his email. Polly replied, discreetly, that she felt it was part of her job to screen out anything that was not essential for him to see. Ty ranted that he would be the decision maker about what he needed to see, and she should make sure she printed and delivered every email he received.

When Ty's buddy sent his next batch of explicit photos, Polly dutifully printed them out along with the rest of Ty's email and made sure to place them on top of the pile, front and center on his desk, in plain view for anyone to see.

When Ty returned to his desk and saw what he had been missing, well, let's just say he felt like a part of the anatomy on view in those pictures.

TIPS

This Is Why You Need a Personal Email Address

Don't use your work email for communicating with friends. Need I say more?

CASE FILE

A Moving Experience

Mo was making a plan to move on from her current job, taking a position with a competitor that would entail relocation to another city, where the competitor's headquarters were located. It's not uncommon when an employee is leaving for the competition, especially if the competition between companies is fierce, for the employee giving notice to be terminated immediately to avoid her taking company information, client contacts, and so on, with her when she defects. Mo knew that, so she was keeping things under her hat while she planned for the big move.

But "under her hat" didn't exclude using her office computer during lunch to list furniture on Craigslist that she didn't intend to haul cross-country; sell things on eBay to clear out clutter before the move; and research neighborhoods and apartments in her soon-to-be new city.

Once again, I remind you that nothing you do on a work computer is private, and sure enough, someone who was monitoring web traffic saw all Mo's activity. Combined with a recent job listing in an industry publication for someone with Mo's background, management put the pieces together. All of a sudden, Mo found herself with plenty of free time to plan the move.

TIPS

Discretion Is the Better Part of Valor

Things that you shouldn't share with your employer by posting or pursuing them at work:

- Your future job plans
- What you're getting everyone for Christmas
- Where you're taking the family on vacation
- What you did with your friends last Saturday night

CASE FILE

Bandwidth Cap

A young employee named Van liked movies. He liked movies a lot. But he didn't like paying for them, so he downloaded illegal copies of recent films via the internet.

Van knew—because he worked in IT—that his company had a much faster internet connection than he had at home, so he began doing his illegal downloads at the office in the background while he did his usual work. He figured he was safe from being caught because he was in IT—he was the person who was watching everyone else's internet traffic for things they weren't supposed to be doing.

But Van's habit was eating up bandwidth and slowing everyone else down. His boss, the IT manager, started getting flak from management about the crawling internet and its effect on business. The boss asked Van if he had seen anyone doing anything illicit that would account for the problem. Van said no.

But he wasn't wise enough to cut it out. His boss took a look at the activity logs and immediately saw what Van was up to. Van was in other respects a good employee, and his boss decided it was probably a mistake of youth. He reprimanded young Van and told him to cut it out.

Which Van did—for a month or two. Then, when he got tired of waiting for slow downloads at home—or maybe worried about his illegal downloads being tracked to his home IP address—he decided to chance it and download a movie here and there, at times of day when there was little internet traffic and therefore less likelihood he would slow everyone else down and be noticed.

But Van's boss was of the "trust but verify" school of thought. He had flagged any of the relevant traffic to make sure the employee had kept his word and was immediately aware when Van began his downloads again.

Two strikes and Van was out.

TIPS

Risky Business

- Downloading movies, streaming music, watching YouTube videos, or any other bandwidth-intensive activities are likely to be noticed by management. Even if it's business related, it's the kind of thing that is monitored in order to manage resources. So if it's not business related, it's not a good idea.
- Illegal downloads are that much worse; by doing something illegal on the job, you expose your company to risk of legal action. Don't flatter yourself that you're such a key employee that the company would be willing to take that risk. You're not, and they won't.
- Games, whether online or on your office computer, are probably not part of your job, either. Is it really worth risking your job to take a solitaire break? If you have to do it, do it on your phone—as long as it's not a company phone.
- Remember, too, that if you have a company BlackBerry or cell phone, that's a company device, too, and you should observe the same separation between business and personal activities when using that device.
- If you're using your personal device—such as a smartphone—to access business materials, be sure to use a separate account for work email than for personal, so not to muddy the waters. Be careful, too, when sending an email from your phone to note which account you're sending from. It's not uncommon for someone to accidentally send a business

message to a coworker from a personal email account, then have the entire chain of replies go to that account on the phone and be missed when the employee is at his or her desk.

- Many people use a cloud service such as Google Drive or Dropbox to store large business files so they can work on them at home or on the road. Again, it's wise to set up a separate account with those services for your work-related materials. Both of the aforementioned services, and others like them, offer the ability to keep a synchronized folder on your desktop containing all your files; if you're using your personal account and enable that feature, you may not realize that all your personal documents are mirrored on your office computer. Even if your personal documents are innocuous—pictures from your vacation, note to the dog sitter, that novel you've been working on since college—they don't belong on the office computer. And many of us have more personal items, like financial documents or information about our children, stored in a cloud service folder. You definitely don't want that on the office computer, potentially accessible to the company. Use a separate account for work.

Phone Home

Is it okay for your employer to ask for your cell number? Sure, they can *ask*.

Many employers do ask for employees' cell numbers for emergency contact. During Hurricane Sandy, when a large portion of lower Manhattan was essentially closed due to flooding and hurricane-related power outages, businesses whose premises were inaccessible or lacked power contacted employees via cell numbers—since many employees were similarly affected and not at their home numbers—to let them know the situation, advise when the office would reopen, and give directions about working remotely.

Giving your boss your cell number isn't a bad idea, either. If he or she needs to contact you outside office hours, the call won't end up being answered by a family member who forgets to tell you for three days. Also, if it's a genuinely urgent situation—someone is fired while you are on vacation and you're the only other person who knows where the client presentation is—the call will find you quickly.

However, if your boss is of the "you're on call 24/7" school, you might feel less inclined to make yourself so easily available. You can claim you are one of the eleven people left in America without a cell, but when you pull it out to answer a call from your significant other, that game will be up. (Also, you may be labeled a Luddite, stuck in a previous century, which isn't necessarily good for your career.) It's perfectly legitimate to tell your boss you prefer to use the cell for personal matters only because you're on a limited plan or you need to keep your line open for emergency calls from family or you just want to be professional and keep your personal business separate and ask your boss to use the number only in an emergency.

And just because your employer calls your personal phone doesn't mean you have to answer . . .

MEMO TO MANAGEMENT

The more at home employees feel—or the more time they spend at the office—the more likely they will do personal business on company computers. You may not want to be draconian and look the other way at a little logging on to Facebook or checking Gmail, but beware of the slippery slope. Clear boundaries will assure that everyone understands exactly what is acceptable and what is not and make dealing with transgressions much more straightforward.

CHAPTER 4

What Happens in Vegas May Not Stay in Vegas

Keeping Off-Hours Peccadillos Out of the Workplace

Keeping work and private life separate is a good idea, but in this highly connected era, it may be harder than it seems. We've all heard stories of modern-day would-be Ferris Buellers who call in sick but then post to Facebook pictures of themselves at the beach or out partying, setting the post as public or forgetting that they accepted a friend request from a boss or HR rep. I hope you're smart enough not to make that mistake.

But even when your outside activities have nothing to do with work, there may be consequences back at the job. Even during off hours, your job may define you enough that the damage to your personal reputation affects your workplace reputation. Or worse, your company may decide they don't want to be associated with you. And rest assured, what you do on your own time often has a way of finding its way back to the workplace. What happens in Vegas not only may not stay in Vegas—it could cost you your job.

"WHEN HIS BOSS TOLD HIM TO GIVE MORE THOUGHT TO 'CONSTRUCTIVE AND DECONSTRUCTIVE PROBLEM SOLVING', I DOUBT THIS IS WHAT HE HAD IN MIND!"

CASE FILE
Swinging for the Fences

A senior executive we'll call Harry had an ongoing argument with his next-door neighbor. We never did find out what the original beef was, but the neighbors had been sniping back and forth over whatever it was for some weeks. Finally, late one night, aided by an appreciable quantity of whiskey, Harry's temper boiled over.

Wearing only his underwear, Harry grabbed a baseball bat and charged out of his house. He slugged his way through the fence between his and his neighbor's property, then practiced his home-run swing on the neighbor's air-conditioning unit.

Harry's neighbor called the police, who disarmed the drunk and irate executive and took him into custody, charging him with disorderly conduct. His wife was dragged out of bed to bail him out, and he made it to work the next morning, a little late and a little the worse for wear.

That might have been the end of the story, until someone at his company ran across Harry's mug shot on the website of the local sheriff's office—it's not just celebrities whose mug shots are posted online; many communities make them all available. Harry was, shall we say, not looking his best in the mug shot—drunk, sleepy-eyed, unshaven, and shirtless. Hardly the polished professional he was at the office. You won't be surprised to hear that the link to the mug shot traveled far and wide within Harry's company.

Harry was surprised, however, when he went into the coffee room and found his mug shot printed out and posted above the coffeepot.

He's just lucky nobody pulled out a smartphone and put the incident up on YouTube.

TIPS

Taking the Fifth

If you get into legal trouble outside work, should you tell your employer?

Yes, if:

- The transgression is job related. Even if you're innocent, it's better that you alert management—and have the opportunity to make your case—than they find out when the police come around asking questions.
- What you're charged with is something that would have kept you from being hired if it were on your record preemployment—for example, if you work in law enforcement or the financial industry. Similarly, if your company has strict rules about disclosing arrests, and you don't, concealing the situation may be considered equivalent to lying about it.
- It's going to make the papers. Everyone will find out anyway, so a heads-up gives you a chance to do a little damage control.
- The consequences—court appearances, etc.—will require you to take unplanned time off work.

No, if:

- It's a minor matter unrelated to your job. They may or may not find out about your fight with your neighbor, but as long as it's likely to be resolved without consequences to your ability to do your job or your reputation in the company or industry, there's no reason to make it an issue.
- Being presumed guilty—of something you didn't actually do—would affect your ability to do your job. For example, if

you were falsely accused of stealing, you risk your employer thinking you a thief and restricting your access to money or property. If you can clear things up quietly, you don't risk losing responsibility or operating under a cloud of suspicion. Clouds of suspicion don't always go away, even after the charges have. However, if you *did* do the crime, it's a different story.

MEMO TO MANAGEMENT

The employee who posted Harry's mug shot in the coffee room was clearly out of line, but whenever an employee is involved in a legal matter, it is a good idea to manage the message. The employee is presumed innocent until proven guilty, but whatever the situation, if the legal matter doesn't directly affect your business, you'll want to keep the chatter from overwhelming everyone's ability to do their jobs. If you can't keep the entire matter under wraps—and in this day and age, that's virtually impossible—at least make sure any conversations about it are based strictly on facts, that employees at all levels realize that this is not an appropriate subject for gossip, and that everyone knows that discussion or speculation that might affect the company negatively—like telling a customer or client that an employee is out of the office for his court date—may result in disciplinary action.

CASE FILE
End of the Line

A quiet, nerdy guy called Ned was one of those non-descript people you barely notice and barely remember. He spent his workdays hunkered down in his cubicle in his threadbare business shirts, nose to the computer, at a desk that was always clear except for a framed photo of his family and an extra pair of glasses. He was polite and pleasant with colleagues but didn't really talk much about his life outside work.

Ned failed to come into work two days in a row without calling. The first day, he was barely missed; he was so quiet when he was in. By the second day, though, people noticed his absence because the usually reliable Ned had failed to deliver work to others. His manager was about to call his home to check on him when Ned's wife called him in a panic: Was Ned at the office? Had they seen him or heard from him?

It seemed Ned had left home in the middle of the night—and left behind a note for his wife. He had inherited a six-figure sum after the death of a relative, she revealed—shocking enough, given the well-worn state of Ned's clothing, his high-mileage old car, bargain-store tastes, and the absence of any other signs of affluence—but Ned had confessed in his note that he had squandered all the money on strippers and prostitutes he had found online. He ended his note by saying that he couldn't face his family after what he had done and didn't think they would ever want to see him again anyway, so he was going to end his life.

The authorities were of course immediately involved, and they asked that we review the information on the computer that Ned had spent his days focused on. Sure enough, the computer data contained the evidence of his addiction to online pornography—he visited many porn sites daily, all of which required payment to see "the good stuff"—as well as his correspondence with prostitutes in the Elliot Spitzer price range.

This story has a happy ending, however. A few days later, Ned was located alive, hiding out in a motel room a few towns over. He had realized he didn't really want to kill himself, but was too embarrassed and afraid to come back and face his family until police discovered him and he had no choice.

Ned returned to his job—with the condition that he seek therapy for his issues and that certain sites and keywords be blocked on his office computer. He also returned to his family. With the support of family and coworkers, he's putting his life back together.

MEMO TO MANAGEMENT

Discretion in a sad situation like this is key. Whatever the outcome, there is nothing gained in trumpeting an employee's personal issues around the office; better to be supportive of the authorities and the family, while of course assessing any potential risk to the company. In this case, discretion about the circumstances and a compassionate response from management allowed a good employee to return without undue disruption around the office.

CASE FILE
Payback Is a Bitch

Not long ago, we dismissed an employee for cause, and she wasn't happy about it. Nobody's happy about being fired, but this former employee took her anger to frightening extremes.

After her departure, the employee, whom we'll call Toni, began sending text messages to her former supervisor. She called the supervisor a "controlling b****," and blamed her for the issues that led to the dismissal. Toni told her ex-boss that because of the firing, she couldn't feed her family, and she held her supervisor responsible for that. Even after being asked to stop contacting anyone at her former employer, Toni continued the barrage of messages to her former supervisor. She escalated to threatening to commit suicide because of the pain of losing her job. Finally, she told her ex-boss she knew where the boss lived, giving the address and names of the supervisor's family members, and threatened to "go out with a bang" by coming to the workplace or the supervisor's home and taking her and others with her.

We don't take threats of violence—to oneself or to others—lightly. We contacted the authorities immediately, and the former employee was taken into police custody.

It's Not Just Talk

You might be angry about being fired or upset about some other issue or problem at work, but be careful what you say—to colleagues, friends, or online. These days, when hostile and/or mentally ill people have acted on threats to harm or kill too many times, any employer has to take a threat—however idle—very seriously, just in case. A threatening remark made in the heat of anger, whether or not you ever had even a moment's thought of following through, will lead to immediate involvement of police, and if you haven't been fired, there's a good chance you will be.

TIPS

Four Ways to Keep Your Cool

If something at the workplace lights your fuse, here are some ways to blow off steam so you can deal with the situation rationally and keep your job and reputation:

- If you have to rant, rant to a friend or loved one. Don't rant to colleagues, no matter how trusted (alliances shift; also, you might be overheard by someone who doesn't realize you're just getting things off your chest). Definitely don't rant on social media.
- Do something physical: if you have the flexibility to step out for a walk, do that. If you have to stay put, you can still do some jumping jacks or running in place. Burn off some of that negative energy in a healthy way.
- If you just feel like you need to hit something, find a safe way to do that. Wait until you're away from work, and take some swings at a punching bag, or make this the day to knock down that old fence. I heard of a fellow who offered to help a friend with some demolition on his property on the condition he could write his boss's name on the cinderblocks before he took a sledgehammer to them. He felt better, and helped his friend out to boot!
- Maybe there's no one you feel comfortable talking to about the situation. Then take a piece of paper and pour it all out there—how you feel, what you wish you could do, anything you need to get out of your system. Then make sure to destroy the piece of paper. In fact, ripping it up into tiny pieces may be therapeutic in helping you get rid of the anger.

Once you're in a calmer frame of mind, you'll be better equipped to address the issue with a clear head.

MEMO TO MANAGEMENT

If you don't have a policy in place for addressing threats of harm, including threats of suicide, you need one. Everyone should be aware that this is a very serious matter, and even offhand remarks—"I just want to strangle that guy"—should be followed up on. In most cases, it's just talk—but you never want to find out too late that the employee was serious about doing harm. In addition to the potential liability issues, there is the personal: if you realize in the aftermath of a tragedy that you saw and overlooked the signs, you will have to live with that. Better safe than sorry, both legally and morally.

We had two women—different times, different areas of the business—with similar complaints: male coworkers were commenting on their breasts. As we've seen in a previous chapter, that is not work-appropriate conduct. But in both these cases, there was another factor in play.

One woman reported the harassment from one specific coworker. He was brought in to meet with management about the issue, at which point he handed over his cell phone to show the text message exchanges he had been having outside work with the woman. Her messages to him included the following gems:

- "u r a great kisser"
- "you would luv my boobs"
- "my boobs are a perfect 34dd—enjoy!"

He said she was claiming harassment because he hadn't called her back after a recent date. We concluded the situation was consensual and not harassment.

The other woman brought her complaint to the Equal Employment Opportunity Commission that men in the office had been heard discussing her breasts. During the investigation, it came out that the woman had posted a number of nude photos of herself on a provocative website. The EEOC determined that those photos were the subject of the discussion and dismissed the employee's claim.

In both these cases, activity outside the workplace affected the outcome of a claim of sexual harassment in the workplace. In fact, lots of things you do outside work can come back to haunt you when you raise a complaint; for example, you might claim that you've been passed over for a promotion in favor of a less experienced candidate and find that management factored into their promotion decision the fact that you were posting the praises of a competitor's product on Twitter. You don't live, or work, in a vacuum, and neither does your employer.

Gossip has a way of taking on a life of its own. If you've ever played a game of telephone, you know how a message changes with being passed down the line, losing—or gaining, in the case of juicy gossip—in translation. Stories get more colorful and vivid with retelling.

That was the case when two employees were talking about a third in the elevator. "I bet he lives at home with his mother, and still has all his *Star Trek* posters on the bedroom wall," one joked. Another employee boarded the elevator in the course of the conversation. She repeated the remark to someone in her department, and away it went, through the rumor mill. After a few rounds, it had the poor fellow living in a house with his dead mother, à la *Psycho*, and hoarding *Star Wars* action figures that he planned to sell on eBay to pay for his retirement.

Silly gossip, until someone was relating it, to great guffaws, once again in the elevator. Also in the elevator, unrecognized by the gossipers, was the man's wife, who was meeting him for lunch. She was not amused.

The wife was able to describe the storyteller to her husband (who, incidentally, did not live with his mother, living or dead), who spoke to that employee's supervisor about the matter. The storyteller ended up being reprimanded for gossip he didn't even start.

TIPS

Shh! Don't Tell

Gossip is hard to resist, but it's wise to know where to draw the line. A couple things to consider before you share something over coffee:

- Will it affect the person's reputation in the company? If so, he or she might have reason to take it up with HR, and they might in turn take it up with you.
- If it got out, might it affect the company's reputation or business? You might tell people not to tell, but we all know how ineffective that can be in the long run.
- How would you feel if someone said the same thing about you? Good workplace relationships rely on the golden rule.

- Why are you telling this? If the reason is to make yourself look better, or to build a reputation as a raconteur, be aware that it might backfire on you and have the opposite result.

MEMO TO MANAGEMENT

Gossip is virtually impossible to control. It's human nature. Attempting to crush every little bit of chatter is a losing proposition, and will likely only result in everyone being careful that no gossip reaches your ears. (Admit it, you probably enjoy an amusing anecdote as much as the next person.) Focus on the talk that is potentially damaging to the business, and make it clear to your employees that *that* kind of talk is not acceptable.

CHAPTER 5

Crime Doesn't Pay Biweekly

It continues to amaze me how many employees attempt to supplement their paychecks through criminal activity, most commonly by stealing from the company. And it never fails to amaze them how easily they get caught.

Just in case no one has said this to you explicitly: No matter how much time you spend at the office, or how much your employer makes you feel at home, company property (and money) belong to the company, not you. If you are not happy with your compensation for your job, you don't get to solve that by helping yourself to anything on the company dime.

Recently, we audited our accounts and found a problem. A seventy-thousand-dollar problem. Upon further investigation, we discovered that the only person who had had access to those funds—and who had attempted during the investigation to explain it away as a calculation error (because apparently he thought no one else could do arithmetic)—was the chief financial officer, Lou.

In fact, Lou had been funneling funds into personal expenditures to support a luxury lifestyle that included the kind of very expensive bottles of wine that you read about in wine specialist magazines, enough jewelry from Tiffany's to have a stockpile of those signature blue boxes, and elegant designer clothing. Naturally, people knew him as well-turned out, as one would expect of a senior executive, but we didn't realize how well until we saw the numbers.

You won't be surprised—if you've read the previous chapters—that we were able to access his browsing history on his office computer. You won't be surprised—if you've read about stupid crooks before—that our thief-in-chief was making these luxury purchases on the company credit card from his desk in his office during business hours.

The real kicker? He'd started stealing from the company three weeks after he started the job. Pretty much as soon as he got settled in, he started helping himself.

I summoned the thief-in-chief into my office to show him the evidence and give him his walking papers. I also demanded that he pay back the seventy grand immediately.

Lou claimed he didn't have that kind of money—it was all spent. Now if you work in a company of any significant size, you know that chief financial officers aren't earning minimum wage. It's bad enough that he violated the trust placed in him as manager of all the company finances, but he also felt that his already generous salary required supplementing out of company coffers. I told Lou that he could deliver the money to me by Monday morning, or he would find himself wearing a different kind of silver bracelets.

Miraculously, Lou was able to find the money after all. When I walked into the building Monday morning, he was already there waiting, cashier's check for seventy thousand dollars in hand.

MEMO TO MANAGEMENT

In a situation like this, you don't have to offer the employee the opportunity to make restitution in order to keep out of jail, but with such a high-profile employee, it may make sense to do so. The bad press that comes of a senior financial manager tapping the till may reflect poorly on the company's reputation.

A high-level thief may, however, be counting on that. He's figuring he'll get away with a very quiet slap on the wrists and a corporate memo about him departing to "pursue other opportunities." Don't be afraid to involve the authorities if the thief doesn't make things right. There may be a flurry of bad press, but it can be managed by focusing on the fact that your systems were robust enough to catch him, and you are taking action to be sure that the company and its stockholders are compensated for the loss. That will blow over faster than if the crook gets away with it, goes somewhere else and does the same thing, and gets caught and it comes out that he scammed your company as well—right out from under your nose.

CASE FILE

Junk Mail

Not all employee thefts are in such high amounts. Sometimes, it's just a little bit here, a little bit there . . . but eventually it adds up enough for the employee to be caught.

Liz was one such employee. She was an old-timer—in fact, the second employee the company had hired at its founding. As the company had grown, so had her responsibilities, until her title was operations manager.

Employees and colleagues appreciated that Liz, despite advancing, was still hands-on. She wasn't above helping open mail from customers.

What we found out, and confirmed through video surveillance, was that Liz wasn't just pitching in to be a team player. Some of the money coming into the company from customers was disappearing into Liz's pockets.

Needless to say, she was fired.

Motive, Means, and Opportunity

What makes a person do something like this? In many cases, it's simply easy access to money and the thought that it will not be missed. It usually starts as "just this once." That was the case with Liz—we later learned that she had fallen prey to a serious drug addiction. She took a little money at first when she needed a fix "just this once." But it was easy because of her position, and she wasn't caught because it was (initially) a small amount of money--and the monkey was still on her back. Just as the drugs became a habit, the stealing to fund the drugs did, too.

We were never able to find out for sure exactly how long it was going on or how much she stole over the years.

Chief financial officer is a position with a high level of responsibility. With great responsibility comes great temptation, as we've seen. Sometimes, the temptation isn't just to help yourself; it's to help out your friends.

Another financial executive I worked with had control over salaries. The company was riding out difficult financial times (as so many companies have in recent years), and one of the measures in place was a salary freeze. Most employees were understanding of the situation—better to have a job but no raise than to have no job. The best employees know that when the situation improves, they will be rewarded for their hard work to help keep the ship afloat. And if that doesn't happen, once the economic landscape improves, a good professional reputation is a highly marketable commodity.

This financial executive held the line on salaries for everyone. Well, almost everyone. Throughout the freeze, a couple select people, his trusted deputies, found their paychecks a little fatter as the executive unilaterally granted them raises. He was rewarding their personal loyalty to him, and he was confident that they wouldn't tell anyone. He was also assuming no one would notice the salary bumps amid the changes in the overall company salary budget that happen when people leave, temporary help is hired or let go, and so forth.

What he didn't count on was the fact that other people do look at those long, dry, detailed reports that senior managers are required to produce and share with their fellow executives. He assumed his colleagues would focus on the bottom line and leave the minutiae to him.

He assumed wrong.

Like many financial executives, this man was a CPA (certified public accountant), and as a CPA he should have detailed professional knowledge and should observe certain professional ethics and fiduciary responsibilities. He failed to meet the obligations not just of his position but of his profession and lost his job over it.

TIPS
Financial Ethics Test

Whatever your level of responsibility, if you are tempted to do something even a little out of the ordinary, here's a quick set of questions to ask yourself:

- Is it my money or the company's?
- Is there a company policy that covers this? If so, is this in keeping with that policy?
- If someone I hated did this, would I want to rat him or her out?

The last one is often the most helpful. If you'd consider it illicit if that annoying jerk down the hall did it, you shouldn't do it, either.

CASE FILE
Only the Good Fly Coach

It's not just management who travels for work: sales reps, staff who set up or host exhibits at conventions or meetings, personnel sent to other locations for conferences or training, all may find themselves traveling on the company account, hanging on to receipts and filling out expense reports. All but the smallest companies have clear policies on what may or may not be spent during company travel. And virtually every company deals with employees trying to evade the rules.

We had one fellow, a spiritual cousin of luxury-loving Lou whom I will call Todd, who believed business travel was a hardship, and to mitigate the pain and suffering of being away from home, he should have deluxe accommodation on the road. He turned in an expense report that included first-class air travel (at three times the coach fare) and a hotel that cost $850 a night. (The intern who prepared Todd's expense reports for him—obviously, such a delicate flower could not be expected to bear the hardship of doing his own expense report—commented that what the hotel cost for a night was more than she paid for a month's rent.) Yes, there are cities in the world where hotels, even chain hotels, are quite expensive, and we don't expect businesspeople to stay in truck stop motels, but $850 was extremely high for the cities Todd traveled to. He must have had to work hard to find somewhere that pricey. I hope the amenities were worth it, because we asked him to reimburse us for the difference between the standard rate our other traveling employees were paying and the luxury rate he charged to his expense report.

By the way, when Todd was on vacation on his own dime, he paid for the whole trip with frequent flyer miles and guest points from his business travel. That dime of his own? He didn't spend it.

Another manager used the company credit card to buy a pair of airplane tickets to Hawaii. He and his wife were celebrating their anniversary. When it was called to his attention that the company had no business in Hawaii, and his wife was not an employee, he claimed he'd "mistakenly" used the company card to make the purchase and "forgotten" to rectify the mistake and reimburse the company. Funny thing; we discovered the error and brought it to his attention a year later—when he attempted to buy tickets for another trip, this time to the Bahamas.

Another employee followed all the rules for her business trip: cheapest flight, company-approved hotel, no fancy restaurant meals. Unfortunately, she fell asleep by the pool and missed the client meeting she had been sent for. She wasn't with that company much longer.

And then there was the salesman who ordered X-rated pay-per-view movies and charged them on his hotel bill, then stopped by the drugstore for condoms and spent the evening with a fellow sales rep at a strip club—and put it all, neatly documented with receipts, on his expense report as business expenditures. That might have flown if he were in the adult entertainment industry, but not so much in any other business.

Travel Tips

Most companies have policies, as I said, about business travel. These are the most common rules. Your boss or company may be more liberal in certain respects, but err on the side of caution, and you will be valued.

- Flights must be coach for all but the highest-ranking employees, at the cheapest available nonstop fare. Many large companies have an arrangement with a travel agency with whom flights must be booked in order to assure policies are observed. You don't use the company travel agent, you don't get reimbursed.
- Travel is only reimbursed for the time you're there for business. If you decide to take a couple extra days as vacation (with your boss's prior approval) and do a little sightseeing after the business obligations are met, you do that at your own expense. In the old days, flights were much cheaper if you stayed over a Saturday, so some companies would spring

for an extra night or two in a hotel if it was less than what they saved by the employee staying the weekend; these days, Saturday-stay restrictions are all but nonexistent and so are those kinds of negotiations.

- The IRS has a per-diem—daily amount—that one can deduct for meals while traveling for business, which differs based on city. Your company probably has similar limits. Unless you are entertaining business associates (and even then, there are probably guidelines), be modest in your meal expenses. Breakfast, lunch, and dinner are usually fair, but don't be ordering the lobster every night, and don't think the nightcap at a club will be covered.
- It is not your employer's job to buy you clothes, toiletries, and so on. We assume you will pack your own. If you forgot to pack pajamas or underwear and have to run out to buy them, that's at your personal expense. Even if the airline loses your luggage and you have to buy something to get through your meeting, expect to work that out with the airline.
- Incidental office supplies or services (using the hotel printer or fax, for example) that are essential to the business you're there to conduct are generally acceptable expenses. Don't go crazy, though; buy only what you can show was essential to the business you're there to conduct.
- Same goes if you have to pay for internet. Some hotels include wireless internet in the room price; others charge for it, and some charge by the hour or the amount of data. In those cases, you can expect to be reimbursed for internet access that is essential to your work, but if you rack up the hours/megabytes on Facebook updates or watching baby sloths on YouTube. . . . I know the baby sloths are adorable

and a great stress reducer, but they're not a legitimate business expense.

- Any other expenses: Ask yourself if they are essential to the business at hand and are things the company would normally pay for if the business were conducted in the office. If the answer is yes in both cases, but the amount is high, you should probably still clear it with management. Your boss is only a phone call or email away, and if you have documented approval, you won't run into trouble later when you submit your expense report for reimbursement.
- Bottom line: Your business travel expenses should cost less money than the business you're doing makes the company. Otherwise, the company isn't going to be afloat for very long.

MEMO TO MANAGEMENT

A clear, consistent policy regarding business travel expenses—any business expenses, for that matter—is essential. Small companies often feel they don't need to be so formal, but if you decide what is reimbursable case by case, you run the risk of abuse or of employees feeling uncertain and uncomfortable about what is appropriate to spend and what is not. Furthermore, if different managers make different decisions, it's hard to maintain a policy that is evenhanded and fiscally responsible. As noted above, a company that doesn't manage its expenses relative to income generated is going to be in trouble.

CASE FILE
All Work, All the Time

Bella was devoted to her job, no question. She worked long hours and never missed a day and seldom took vacation. We value employees like Bella, but even for someone like her, there are limits to what is an appropriate business expense.

Whenever Bella worked late, she called a car service to take her home. That would be fine if it was a once-in-a-while thing related to a particular deadline or project, but Bella did it so often she was basically commuting via car service. The vice president she reported to asked her to put a stop to that, and she did.

Instead, every time the weather looked even a little dicey ("it's going to snow," "there's a forecast of thunderstorms"), Bella booked a room in the hotel closest to the office and charged it to the company. "I was afraid I wouldn't be able to get into the office in the morning," she explained to her boss.

She also ordered lunch on the company account every day and dinners frequently. "I didn't want to lose any work time, so I ordered in," she said in her defense. That's great, the VP told her, but we pay employees a salary so they can pay for their own meals. No one was ordering her to eat in the office, so if she chose to do that, it would be at her own expense.

"Don't you value my devotion?" Bella asked.

We do, her boss told her, but we show that with salary. Expensing the things that are ordinary living expenses—eating, commuting, having a place to sleep—amounts to supplementing salary without approval. And a good employee would never do that.

Good employee that she was, Bella saw it his way. And she sometimes went home at a decent hour, which was probably healthy for her, too.

CASE FILE
Wiped Out

Lots of employees seem to think that office supplies are free for their personal use. Pens, paperclips, Post-Its, note pads all go home with people all the time, sometimes inadvertently and frequently intentionally. Wonder why your company buys cheap pens and off-brand supplies? Partly to save money and partly to make them less enticing to thieves. Nicer pens get "used up" at a surprisingly rapid rate compared to cheap stick pens.

Employees have taken home hanging folders and tabs in order to file their tax materials, colored markers to label things around the house, paper for their home printer, spiral notebooks and pencils for their children to use for school, and whiteboard erasers to use with a whiteboard in their kitchen. I heard of an employee who was strapped for cash and stole the milk employees were using for their coffee. But the one I'll never forget is the toilet paper thief.

The office manager noticed that the toilet paper in the ladies' room was running out frequently, and she was always having to call the custodial staff to bring more. Someone would bring up a bunch of rolls and leave extra rolls in each stall. But this was happening day after day. Was there something in the water? Unless the female employees were having a sudden excessive need of toilet paper, something was up.

Sometimes, when something goes missing, a company will install cameras to watch the item in question. Cameras in the rest room, however, would present a violation of privacy (not to mention an opportunity for abuse), so that was off the table. Many women went into the bathroom with large bags—backpacks, tote bags—when they were on their way out at the end of the day, any of which could easily have stashed away a roll or two. But we were seeing more than one or two rolls disappear. So the office manager kept her eye out for someone with a larger than average bag who took that bag into the rest room in the middle of the day when we were most frequently getting the out-of-paper complaints.

It wasn't long before she zeroed in on a staffer who went to the gym during lunch with a large gym bag. Sure enough, the bag seemed fuller when she returned to her desk after lunch than when she'd left for the gym—whether or not *she* was bulking up with her workouts, her bag sure was. The employee was confronted.

Who needs that much toilet paper? It turned out the employee's best friend had opened a small café, and our employee was helping out there after hours. Our employee was stealing supplies for the café rest room, as well as other office supplies (in smaller, less noticeable quantities) as her way of pitching in.

She was very soon free to work full-time at her friend's café.

TIPS

Look but Don't Take

Office supplies and equipment belong to the company, not you. Use them for your work. Use them at the office. Don't use them for personal stuff, and don't take them with you when you leave the premises. It may seem small or innocent enough to take a few folders or pens, but if someone is looking to make trouble for you, they can point to those few items and cry thief, and there's not much you can do to defend yourself.

MEMO TO MANAGEMENT

How you keep and dispense office supplies conveys a message about them and can help prevent shrinkage. Office supplies kept in large quantities in easily accessible areas give the message that they are ubiquitous, cheap, and nothing will be missed. Even if you order in large quantities to realize cost savings, it's advisable to keep the large quantities in storage space and make only limited numbers of items available at once. Also, keeping bulk supplies in a secured area, even if it's just inside someone's office, gives the message that they are valuable. Most office supply theft occurs because people think of the supplies as "nothing." Change the perception, and employees will think twice about walking away with the company's property, however small.

CASE FILE
Super Bowl Shuffle

The 1985 Chicago Bears rapped that they weren't there to make any trouble, but the Super Bowl sure caused some trouble for purchasing manager Frankie.

Frankie worked with a wide variety of vendors, purchasing numerous items in significant quantities for a manufacturing operation. A big part of his job was establishing strong relationships with his vendors so that they understood the company's business and were able to anticipate and accommodate seasonal and other needs, and so that Frankie could negotiate the best possible prices. Frankie was a big buyer—if he moved all the company's business from one vendor to another, it could make a big difference in that vendor's bottom line—so they had a big incentive to keep Frankie happy.

Frankie was happy when vendors delivered high-quality product on time, within the price guidelines, because that made Frankie look good to his bosses, and he was duly rewarded when raise time came. But lots of good vendors were capable of doing that, so some of them sought an edge.

It's common for vendors to pick up the tab for lunch with a customer like Frankie, or send a big box of Christmas cookies around the holidays. But many companies, especially those with larger budgets, have policies limiting what an employee can accept from a vendor to prevent a purchasing manager like Frankie being bribed to make a decision not in the company's best interest, like, for example, accepting sub-standard materials or doing business with a company that wasn't offering the best price.

One of Frankie's vendors had a sales rep who'd worked with Frankie for many years. He knew that Frankie loved football, and when his team made it to the Super Bowl, the vendor rep saw an opportunity to cement his company's place in Frankie's business plan—he offered Frankie a pair of tickets to the Super Bowl. Good seats, too, that were selling online for five figures.

When Frankie returned to the office after the big game, he couldn't stop talking about what a great time he'd had and how great the seats had been. He didn't mention how he'd come by those seats, but when the same vendor made a similar offer of concert tickets to another purchasing manager, we put two and two together and had a little chat with Frankie.

Yeah, he'd accepted the tickets from the rep, he admitted, but claimed the rep was offering them not as a business associate but as a friend. Unfortunately, the seats were part of the vendor company's season ticket package—they were clearly the property of the vendor, not the rep, and clearly from the business. Frankie had to have known that even a good friend doesn't usually have tickets in that price range he or she can afford to hand out.

Although there was no evidence Frankie had changed his ordering patterns as a result of receiving the Super Bowl tickets, he was clearly afoul of company policies about accepting gifts from vendors and was disciplined accordingly.

CASE FILE
Naked Capitalism

Frankie was blinded to the ethics of his situation by his desire to go to the Super Bowl, but he was basically a good employee who made a bad choice. Nick was a different sort.

Nick made it clear to his vendors that if they expected his business, he expected some perks in return. "It's just the capitalist system at work," he told one of them.

That led to his vendors offering him a variety of so-called incentives in order to get and keep his business. The winning "bidder" paid for repeat business from Nick by hosting wild nights at strip clubs, in which large quantities of alcohol were consumed. Just to seal the deal, the vendor made sure Nick had all the lap dances and other favors from the strippers he wanted, all on the vendor's tab.

The vendor considered this the cost of doing business. We found out when a competing vendor cried foul. Ultimately, the wild nights cost the "winning" vendor the company's business and cost Nick his job.

TIPS

Look a Gift Horse in the Mouth

Giving or receiving, you can get yourself in trouble if you aren't careful about gifts or favors in the working world.

Before you accept something—gift, meal, entertainment—from someone you or your company deals with, ask yourself:

- Does my employer have a policy about what I can accept? Does this run afoul of that policy?
- Do I have any influence over business with this person or company? Even if your role is small potatoes—hiring a temp now and again or buying small items when your workplace runs out—the possibility of influence exists.
- Might the giver think I have influence over company spending? Even if you don't have any role in purchasing decisions, a vendor may not realize that and may be seeking to influence you. That can still get you in trouble—as well as souring the company's relationship with the vendor when he or she finds out you implied a role you don't have.
- What's the value of the gift? Lunch at a modestly priced place is one thing and not as likely to be perceived as swaying you in the same way as taking you to four-star restaurants and throwing in an expensive bottle of wine.

If you are in a position to give to someone you do business with:

- Keep the price modest. Holiday gifts of food items meant to be shared with the whole office are generally appropriate as a thank-you for the year's business, but expensive gifts to decision makers may cross a line.
- Does the recipient company have a policy about what an employee can accept? Large companies may send vendors a letter clarifying their limits, and if the gift you envision is generous, it's not inappropriate to query the recipient. That will prevent putting him or her in a difficult situation if you send something he or she can't accept without violating company rules.
- Overseas business relationships are a whole 'nother can of worms. In some countries, it's customary to grease palms to get anything done. But in the United States, we call that bribery. Particularly if you are dealing with foreign government officials—at any level from president to dogcatcher—you may be subject to the provisions of the Foreign Corrupt Practices Act of 1977. Consult with appropriate counsel in your company before you make any missteps.

CASE FILE

How the Grinch Bought Christmas

In some companies, it's common for employees to buy a little something for their boss at the holidays. Some bosses like to thank their employees with a holiday gift. In either case, this is a personal choice . . . and a personal expense.

One boss wanted to buy the affection of his staff with nice holiday gifts. Other bosses might give a small box of cookies or a modestly priced bottle of wine. But Greg wanted to be seen as the best boss to work for, so he went the extra mile. He bought individually selected gifts for everyone in his chain of command, none of them ridiculously extravagant but still chosen to build his reputation for generosity. For example, he bought one fellow a silk necktie featuring a design from a famous painting. Greg's staff were indeed impressed, both with the thought that went into the gifts and with the generosity each represented. Other managers noticed, too, and weren't thrilled that Greg was making them look cheap.

Greg, on the other hand, wasn't too happy when his expense report was rejected. He had, it seems, assumed that as the gifts were for employees, they were a legitimate business expense and would be paid for by the company.

I hope he got a lot of mileage out of the gratitude of his staff that year, because they were bound to be disappointed the next year when he was spending his own money.

Another employee at another company attempted to expense his contribution to his boss's Christmas gift—the boss who owned the company and signed his expense reports.

CASE FILE

The Grass Is Greener on the Other Side of the Cubicle Wall

Abuse of alcohol and other substances while at work is a common problem: employees imbibing over lunch and sleeping it off behind a closed office door in the afternoon; salespeople taking customers out for a night on the town and getting hammered; employees sneaking a chemical pick-me-up in the company bathroom. Needless to say (I hope),

"WELL, THEY DO SAY THE GRASS IS GREENER ON THE OTHER SIDE."

drinking, drugs, and doing your job seldom mix. And if you get caught, there's a good chance you will be fired on the spot.

One employee who we'll call Mary Jane—for reasons that will soon become obvious—had a resourceful streak. She and some of her young colleagues had been known to partake of certain illicit substances, but that could get costly on their entry-level paychecks. Many employees livened up the surroundings in their cubicle farm with plants and other greenery, so Mary Jane did the same. The difference was, in among her cluster of coleus and spider plants, she was growing grass—and I don't mean the kind in your lawn.

Mary Jane and her young friends counted on the old fogies being blind to her special plants. She didn't realize that marijuana has been around a lot longer than these twenty-something employees. A more senior staffer, who had his own experiences with the weed back when the Grateful Dead were all alive and the Rolling Stones were still young, immediately recognized what Mary Jane was growing and warned her to get rid of it.

Not one to throw out perfectly good pot, Mary Jane decided to take the plants home. Unfortunately for her, without the protective cover of the other plants that she'd had surrounding it, the plant's identity was obvious to anyone who'd ever seen so much as a picture of the leaf, and word spread—like smoke—in her wake as she carried her plant toward the door. There was quite an audience when the security guard stopped her and asked her to wait for the police.

It might seem excessive for a company to call the police, but Mary Jane put the company at risk by having this illegal substance on company premises. If management took it from her, that person would be at risk of prosecution for possession, and if they simply let her toss it in the Dumpster outside, it's possible someone would find it, and the company would likely face a visit from the police, anyway.

CASE FILE

Do Not Pass Go, Do Not Collect $200

We've had our share of visits from the police—not always because we've called them. More than once, the police have shown up at our doorstep to pick up an employee for a transgression outside of work.

Dave was one example. Dave and his wife had divorced some years earlier, and despite collecting a decent paycheck for his work for our company, he hadn't been paying court-ordered child support. I don't know what Dave's reasons were for avoiding that responsibility, and neither did the court; he'd failed to show up for a court date about the matter. And that led the judge to sign an order for his arrest.

Officers arrived at our front desk and asked for Dave. When the receptionist called his extension and wouldn't, at the officers' request, say who was there to see him, he claimed to be unavailable. Human Resources and company security were alerted, and the officers were shown directly to Dave's desk, where he proceeded to attempt to evade them by pretending to be another employee.

Naturally, our personnel knew who he was and were able to confirm his identity. Then he claimed not to be the correct Dave—that there was some other person with his name who was the subject of the court order. Unfortunately for him, Dave had been very vocal around the office all through the course of his acrimonious divorce; everyone knew he had been fighting with his wife about the child support. Dave was perhaps not at his sharpest in thinking that one was going to fly.

When Dave finally left with the officers, he did so in handcuffs, thanks to his efforts to evade arrest.

Go Directly to Jail

That's far from the only time an employee has been arrested on company premises. The most common reasons are domestic, like Dave's case, but we've also had employees collared for drunk driving, domestic abuse, and even one nice, clean-cut fellow who was arrested for attempted murder. We've also had visits from police to interview employees about events they may have witnessed or people they had information about, just like you've seen on *Law & Order*, and we get regular visits from process servers bringing papers about divorces, lawsuits, and similar matters.

Companies will just about always cooperate with police. It is in the company's best interest to establish and maintain a good relationship with them for the protection of the company's personnel, customers, and property. So even if you are completely blameless in an incident, if the police come calling, don't expect the company to side with you or protect you. Sure, there may be the occasional situation in which management is trying to protect a high-level executive or avoid bad publicity, but those are rare. Most companies would rather let the police take care of their business with the minimum of fuss and disruption and get the problem off their premises.

And no company will reward an employee for behavior that brings the police to their doorstep. Even if the alleged crime has nothing to do with the employee's work or performance, a visit from the heat is, as we saw in Dave's case, an unwelcome interruption and a distraction from work well after the police have gone.

CASE FILE
Sugar, Sugar

Certain industries were hot, hot, hot back in the seventies and eighties. Books have been written and movies made about the excesses on Wall Street, for example. The culture was anything goes.

What went on at one company was a lot of cocaine. One star sales rep was known to excuse himself to "get a little sugar for my coffee," and step into the conference room to use the polished surface of the table to snort lines of cocaine. Everyone knew what he was doing; the conference room had glass walls.

The thing that finally got him in trouble? He expensed a plane ticket to see a client but never turned up at the client's office. Instead, he'd exchanged the ticket for one to the Caribbean and spent three days on the beach working on his tan and his high.

TIPS
Up in Smoke

Question: When are illegal drugs in the office okay?

Answer: Never. Even if you claim you needed them to do your job—as, for example, some long-distance truckers have said about amphetamines to keep awake—the company will always distance itself from illegal conduct. Even if someone in the chain of command knew and was looking the other way, the employee who gets caught is getting thrown under the bus.

Question: What about prescription drugs, including medical marijuana?

Answer: If your prescribed medications don't interfere with your ability to do your job, you should be able to take them. However, if you are using marijuana for a legitimate medical need under a doctor's supervision, you still may run afoul of company policies, for example, about smoking. It's best to discuss the issue with human resources to make sure there will be no problems.

Question: Is it any of my employer's business if I like to have a couple beers at lunch, if I do it off-site?

Answer: If you're of legal drinking age and it doesn't interfere with your ability to do your job, probably not. But if there is the slightest sign of it affecting your job or workplace—if you smell like beer, giving a poor impression to colleagues or customers—you may find yourself in trouble. This is particularly true if any aspect of your work might involve risk of damage or injury, such as if you operate equipment or drive a vehicle. Even if you're not impaired, the suspicion of impairment might be enough to cost your job.

Your employer may have an explicit zero-tolerance policy, too, even if there's no concrete risk involved. Best to have those beers after hours.

Question: One of the managers likes to open a bottle of whiskey after five in his office. I can't get in trouble if I go have a drink there, because he's management, right?

Answer: Not so fast. While the manager bears responsibility for his conduct, that doesn't excuse you if you know, for example, that the company has a policy against alcohol on premises or if you are not of legal drinking age. The company is likely to frown on something like this in any case because of the risk of liability if someone over-consumes and is injured as a result on the way home.

MEMO TO MANAGEMENT

Small companies may be casual about alcohol in the office, in particular—but remember that if you're successful, you won't be at a small company forever. Do you want to set a precedent that will be problematic later?

Moreover, as noted above, if the company is responsible in any way for the drinking—whether it be by hosting an event where alcohol is served, or simply looking the other way while employees have an after-hours drink in the office—the company may be liable for any negative consequences, such as accidents by impaired drivers, alcohol-fueled sexual harassment, or damage to property by drunk employees.

This is another case in which a clear, explicit written policy made available to and acknowledged by all employees is very valuable in preventing a problem and in addressing it if it does occur.

CHAPTER 6

Take Cover

When Employees (and Others) Lose It

The phrase "going postal" entered the lexicon in the early 1990s after a series of well-publicized events in which postal workers shot and killed colleagues and others, most notably the 1986 Edmond, Oklahoma, shooting in which fourteen people were killed and six injured. We've taken a light tone to this point, but the extreme anguish and/or mental illness that might lead someone to such an extreme action is hardly restricted to post office employees, and the risk must be taken very seriously.

The good news is that your odds of dying at the hands of a disgruntled coworker are much less than the risks you face from everyday activities like driving to work. Your safety is even more secure if you and your company watch for signs of trouble and respond soon enough to avert disaster.

Employees, of course, aren't the only workplace risk: customers, clients, visitors, or others may also present a risk to you and your colleagues.

Laws and customs regarding weapons in the workplace vary from place to place, and requirements and standard practices will obviously differ by industry. An angry or mentally unstable person looking to lash out may use whatever is on hand. If weapons or hazardous materials are integral to your work, it's wise to secure them or limit access to avoid access by unauthorized personnel and to minimize the chance of an impulse crime.

The same is true for items that aren't weapons but might be used by a person inclined to cause harm. These are generally items that are also potentially dangerous in terms of accidents—even more reason to be sure they are properly stored and managed. In addition to the risk to everyone's personal safety, the company and its employees (meaning you) may incur liability if careless handling of dangerous items results in injury or death, accidental or intentional.

CASE FILE

Burning Down the Spouse

Domestic disputes can boil over into the workplace with devastating consequences. You need only look to the news for stories of angry spouses or spurned lovers showing up at workplaces with guns or knives. Emotions run high in domestic disputes, and these kinds of situations can be very volatile as a result.

The wife of an employee showed up at our company looking for her husband. Sensing her anger, the security officer at the front desk declined to let her in. He contacted the employee, who explained that they were going through an acrimonious divorce, and the officer was right to bar her entrance.

The wife was not happy when she was asked to leave the premises. She shouted and made a scene and declined to leave. In the course of this, she claimed to be armed and threatened to burn down the building and everyone in it just to get to her husband.

Trespassing would have been sufficient cause to escort her from the premises, but as soon as the threat of violence arose, the security staff felt it necessary to involve the police to be safe.

Fortunately, she wasn't armed, but if she had been, the consequences could have been dire. The woman was removed from the building in handcuffs.

TIPS

Safe from Home

Domestic and relationship-related abuse and violence is terrifyingly common. Note these stats:

- According to the American Bar Association, about 1.3 million women and 835,000 men are physically assaulted by an intimate partner every year in the United States.
- The Department of Justice reports that, in a study of recent offenders, half of all perpetrators in state prison for spousal abuse killed their victim. Women represent the majority—81%—of spouses killed.
- The Stalking Resource Center says 1,006,970 women and 370,990 men are stalked annually in the United States. Stalkers are persistent; the average stalker sticks with his victim for close to two years.
- Same-sex couples aren't safe from domestic violence, either. The National Violence Against Women Survey found that 11 percent of lesbians and 15 percent of gay men reported being victimized by a same-sex partner.

These incidents are more common than you may have realized. That's a good reason to take the risk seriously and use caution when hostility at home overflows into the office.

TIPS

If You Need Help

If you are in immediate danger, call 911. Here are some additional resources, available nationwide, to help you find safety if you or someone you know is experiencing domestic violence. There may also be state and local organizations in your area who can help you.

- National Coalition Against Domestic Violence: 1-800-799-7233 (SAFE); www.ncadv.org/
- Rape, Abuse & Incest National Network (RAINN): 1-800-656-4673; www.rainn.org/

MEMO TO MANAGEMENT

Domestic issues may seem like they are not your problem, but it's too easy for them to spill into the workplace as we've seen time and time again. Employees at risk require your support. Make sure your human resources staff are receptive to employees who are under threat, being stalked, or otherwise at risk. It's not your company's job to resolve the dispute, but the safety of your company, your premises, your employees, your customers, and your guests are most certainly your business, and it is in your best interest to be aware of and prepared for any potential threat.

CASE FILE
Off the Leash

It's not unheard of for employees, especially young ones looking to build a nest egg, to find second jobs for evenings and weekends. One young woman who worked in our sales department during the day, whom we'll call Nancy, did exactly that as she and her husband saved up to buy a home. The outside job that fit her talents and schedule was working as a stripper.

It didn't take long before some of the guys in sales found out about Nancy's other gig. Being the curious young men they were, they had to go see her shake what the Lord gave her. In fact, they became regulars at her strip club and talked about it often. Nancy was the star of the office.

Nancy's husband was as protective as a pit bull, and he was not okay with the guys from the office coming to see her so often. He began phoning Nancy's male colleagues at the office and telling them to stop coming to the club. He threatened some of the men, saying that if they didn't stay away from Nancy at her other job, he would come down to the office and "beat the s***" out of them.

The threats became so frequent and so violent that one of Nancy's coworkers was genuinely afraid and brought the issue to HR. We met with Nancy and explained that what she did on her own time was her own business, but now that her husband's jealousy was spilling over into the workplace, she had better get him on a tighter leash, or we would have to take action.

She managed the situation and was able to keep her second job.

At least the guys from the office tipped well!

TIPS

A Little on the Side

Some companies have policies limiting or prohibiting employees from taking other jobs. Limitations may be on the number of hours or type of outside work the employee does, or the employee may be required to clear the second job with management.

These rules, when they are in place, are to prevent the side job from interfering with the employee's productivity at the main job because he or she is overtired. There may also be restrictions in place that prevent conflicts of interest—such as doing work for a competitor or for a company your company does business with.

Companies will generally make employees aware of any policies relating to outside jobs at hiring. Be sure you abide by such policies. Even if your other job is as innocuous as working at Starbucks, you could put your primary job at risk if your boss stops by for coffee and catches you.

CASE FILE
Conscientious Objector

A law firm represented a company in a sexual harassment suit against a former employee of the company. The employee lost the suit, and along with it his job, and eventually his wife, who was not pleased with the behavior that came out in the trial.

Long after the court case was done, the man showed up at the law firm's offices and began a daily ritual of picketing outside as employees of the law firm came and went. He shouted at the lawyers and their staff about how they had ruined his life and asked how they could sleep at night working for a firm that would defend a company against him and do him so much harm. (Never mind the harm that he did to the victims of his harassment and to the company as a result of his behavior.) His picketing devolved into shouting obscenities at employees. Eventually, the firm obtained a restraining order against the harassing picketer to keep him a safe distance away from its employees and clients.

CASE FILE
Bombshell Offer

Direct mail offers and solicitations are ubiquitous. We all get them every day, and they're probably what's keeping the post office afloat these days. You might call them junk mail, but the fact is, if they didn't work, the companies sending them wouldn't still be investing millions of dollars in these mailings. But that doesn't mean they don't irritate the hell out of some people.

One recipient of a mailing was particularly aggrieved. He phoned our company to say that he had planted bombs in our offices, and if he received another direct mail solicitation from us, he would detonate them. "F*** you, b****" was his closing to the call.

Of course, to make sure we knew who to take off our mailing list in order to save ourselves from harm, he gave his name.

Between that and caller ID, we were able to identify the person making the threat and supply that information to the police.

He claimed he was just angry and there were no bombs, but we and the authorities did check our facilities carefully to be sure. And despite the absence of any real bombs, the customer was prosecuted for making the bomb threat.

TIPS

On Call: Handling Telephoned Threats

Irate or imbalanced people might use any company number to make contact, so no matter what your job, there is a chance you might be the one who picks up the phone when someone calls in a threat of harm. Here's what to do:

- Take all threats seriously. Even if it seems like someone just blowing off steam, don't take a chance. If the caller says he or she might do any kind of harm, they've crossed the line well past simple complaining. Sure, it's probably nothing—but what if it isn't?
- Write down any information the caller supplies. Don't count on remembering what he or she said. If you have caller ID available, write down the caller ID information, too. Make

a note of the time the call came in. Supply all your notes to management and/or law enforcement.

- Contact appropriate personnel immediately. If you don't know who that is, talk to your supervisor or head of security. If a supervisor brushes it off but you think there might be something to the threat, work your way up the line. Trust your gut. Better to cry wolf and be wrong than be silenced and someone gets hurt.
- If there's an imminent threat, call 911. If a specific location was named for the threat, for example "There's a bomb in the loading dock," clear that area immediately and let trained law enforcement professionals look for the bomb.

MEMO TO MANAGEMENT

Employees in customer-facing positions—customer service, reception/switchboard, order takers, and so on—should be trained in how to respond to a telephoned threat. Most threats are idle, but in the rare event that one is not, vital minutes can be lost while the person receiving the call recounts the story to a couple coworkers, wondering whether he or she should say or do anything about it, and vital information may fail to be collected and conveyed if employees have no idea what to do.

There's no need to make employees fearful; just make it part of your routine training in how to deal with an unhappy or angry caller.

FOR HAROLD IT WAS THE 6,529TH DIRECT MAIL LETTER THAT PROVED TO BE THE STRAW THAT BROKE THE CAMEL'S BACK.

CASE FILE
Baby Fresh

It's becoming a common response to direct mail solicitations for recipients who don't want to hear from a company to stuff the postage-paid return envelope with miscellaneous items, most often the torn-up solicitation. It doesn't get you off anyone's mailing list, but maybe it makes some people feel better.

An angrier-than-average recipient decided, in the wake of the anthrax mailings some years ago, to send a company a little bit of white powder to express his outrage. He didn't mean any real harm, just wanted to cause some disruption.

Fortunately, the telltale aroma of the white powder he used helped to identify it—it was baby powder (other eager beavers have even tried flour). The only danger was spilling it on a dark pair of trousers.

Unfortunately for the sender, it is a federal crime to send something dangerous or threatening (even if the threat is fake) through the US mail, so the FBI was involved. The irate sender was no doubt impressed with the quick response to his mailing—it just wasn't at all the response he expected.

TIPS
Thinking Inside the Box

When you were a child, you probably enjoyed feeling birthday or holiday gifts to try to guess by weight and shape and size and sound what was inside before you were allowed to open them. Maybe you honed your technique and got good at guessing.

Identifying a hazardous package before opening it requires a different approach. The United States Post Office has solid advice. The post office notes the following as potential red flags:

- No return address or ambiguous return address. The sender is perhaps trying to remain anonymous.
- Misspelled words, badly written/typed address, and/or sent to a title rather than a name. There are always people who can't spell, who have bad handwriting, or who don't bother to find out the name of a manager before writing, but coupled with other red flags, these could be clues to trouble.
- Restrictive markings such as "personal" or "do not X-ray." May be intended to make sure the package is opened by a specific individual or to slip through normal screening.
- Envelope sealed with tape or package sealed with excessive amount of tape. If there's something toxic inside an envelope, one assumes the sender doesn't want to lick it. Also, the sender might be making sure nothing escapes to be detected in transit.
- Excess postage. Sender wants to make sure it gets to the intended target.
- Sent from a foreign country. May be a foreign threat or someone trying to hide from US authorities.
- Unknown or suspicious powder or other substance on or in the mailing. Anthrax is the best known threat, thanks to the 2001 mailings that killed five people.
- Strange odor or residue. Again, this may indicate something out of the ordinary inside.
- Protruding wires.

And here's what the post office instructs if you receive a suspicious package:

- Stop. Don't handle it.
- Isolate the package immediately, away from people who can be harmed.
- Don't open it, smell it, or taste it. (I hope that last one would go without saying!)
- Notify a supervisor and activate your company's emergency plan. (This should be a reminder to make sure your company has such a plan, and that you know what it is.)

If you suspect the presence of a bomb, or a biological, chemical, or radiologic hazard:

- Isolate the area immediately.
- Call 911.
- Wash your hands with soap and water.

For more information, go to www.usps.com.

MEMO TO MANAGEMENT

Most crackpots are just that—crackpots angry about something looking to make mischief. They're usually not dangerous. However, it's in your best interest to guard against the one or two who might represent a legitimate threat.

Just as with telephone threats, employees receiving or handling mail and packages should be trained in how to identify and handle a potentially threatening or hazardous envelope or package. The guidelines above are helpful, and you may identify specifics appropriate to the nature of your industry and the type of mail and packages you normally receive.

If you are in an industry with a high risk or your company is involved in a high-profile controversy, extra caution may be called for. If the company has received any kind of threats, you and your staff should be especially vigilant. In that case, alert local law enforcement, who can supply guidance on the safest course of action to identify and avert danger.

Similarly, when there have been newsworthy attacks elsewhere, whether or not they target your business or industry, it's wise to alert everyone to be on the lookout for anything outside the norm; there's always a possibility the news coverage will give an upset or unstable person the idea for a copycat crime.

Again, the risk is probably low in most workplaces, so there is no need to instill fear—but healthy caution can prevent harm in that one-in-a-million case.

CASE FILE
Kickass Salespeople

Salespeople who work on commission may make more money, if they are very good at selling, than their salaried managers. When the salesperson is arrogant and obnoxious about that fact, as was the case with one of our salespeople, the situation can get very tense.

Our salesman, Al, liked to flaunt his success. His manager, Phil, took that amiss, and micromanaged Al. Al didn't take kindly to that, and ignored and derided his boss. It was no secret there was no love lost between these two.

What started as taunts back and forth continued in a series of particularly nasty text messages over one weekend. Finally, on Monday morning, Phil met up with Al in the parking lot and picked up the text altercation in person. Words got increasingly heated as the men entered the building and escalated to punches in view of several other employees. Before the two were separated, Phil had a broken nose.

You might think Al would be the one to lose his job in this situation. But investigation—reviewing the text messages, interviewing the witnesses—proved that Phil had started the argument, Phil had pursued it, and Phil had thrown the first punch.

So Phil got the pink slip. Aggressive Al, true to his nickname, didn't let it go at that. He took Phil to court for assaulting him.

Let's end this chapter on a lighter note.

If the long arm of the law is looking to find someone, the most obvious place to look is at the person's home. But during the workday, the obvious place is the person's employer.

More than once, we have had process servers show up at the office to deliver legal notices of lawsuits of various kinds, divorce and family-related matters being the most common among those. When a process server delivers legal papers, he or she is obligated to hand the materials directly to the person who is being sued or subpoenaed. If the recipient knows the summons is coming, he or she might go to great lengths to avoid being found.

A man whom we'll call Carlo was being sued for libel by a notoriously litigious rival, so it was no surprise to Carlo that a process server might be seeking him out. Initially, he asked the receptionist and other coworkers to cover for him, claiming he was not in the office.

But process servers can be very persistent; even more than postal workers, their credo is that neither rain nor sleet—nor a stern receptionist—keeps them from doing their jobs. In this case, the process server situated himself outside the company entrance to wait Carlo out, for as long as it took.

After a couple days, the process server realized Carlo had to be coming and going via another entrance and started watching other places Carlo might be, including a party hosted by a senior executive at his home.

But Carlo was a step ahead of him. He alerted his boss to the situation and arrived in a van hours before the party, dressed as a workman setting up for the event. Once inside the boss's house, he changed clothes and enjoyed the party with everyone else. Then he changed back into costume, helped with the cleanup, and left with a bag of trash in hand.

The matter was eventually settled, and Carlo was able to resume his normal routine and wardrobe. Too bad—a female coworker had offered to lend him a wig and heels if he needed another disguise.

CHAPTER 7

A Straight Flush

Bathroom and Other Personal Fouls

Given the number of hours we all spend in our workplaces, it's practically like sharing an apartment. We share workspace, often in close quarters, we share break or lunch rooms, communal kitchens . . . and bathrooms. And having a messy or thoughtless coworker can be even worse than a nightmare roommate. At least in the case of an awful roommate, you're asleep for some of the time you're in the shared space, and you can leave if you need to. Not so at the workplace; you're stuck there during your scheduled working hours, and sleeping on the job is generally frowned upon.

On the other hand, considerate colleagues can make even the most tedious workplace a little more bearable, and if the job itself is a satisfying one, thoughtful coworkers can make it downright delightful.

Just keep in mind with regard to how you treat your common workspace: your mother doesn't work here . . . but you practically live here.

CASE FILE
Pooper Towels

We had a horrifying instance in which someone had set a trap by opening up the paper towel dispenser in the women's room and placing the product of their bowels inside. Eventually, someone would pull out a paper towel . . . and the you-know-what would drop into her hand. Revolting, to say the least.

We could only imagine the offender fishing her turds out of the toilet, waiting for the bathroom to be empty, then skulking over to the sink and unscrewing the top of the dispenser, removing some towels, and making her deposit, putting some more towels in on top to disguise the evidence, then screwing the dispenser back together before washing up (one hopes!) and heading back to work.

Antibacterial soap for everyone!

You've got to be really crazy to go to that much trouble to do something that disgusting. We reviewed our personnel rosters for signs pointing to that kind of crazy and came up empty.

We decided to send a memo to all our employees, each individually addressed to get their attention, describing the episode and asking for any information. Although the problem was restricted to the women's restroom, we didn't exclude the men from the mail blast, just in case it was a male employee sneaking in to get some kind of revenge on the women, or in case one of the fellows had heard something useful.

All but three of our employees responded immediately with disgust, horror, and the assurance that they knew nothing about it and hoped no one thought they did.

One of the three who had not responded was male, and although, as I said, we considered it possible that a man could be the culprit, we thought it less likely, since a guy coming out of the ladies' room would be noticed, and we might have heard something from someone to that effect. So we focused our attention on the two women who hadn't responded to the personal memo.

One said she hadn't responded simply because she didn't have any information to offer, and like everyone, she thought the whole situation was appalling.

The other woman, a fifteen-year veteran of the company, initially said she had nothing to do with it either, but there was something about her protestation that didn't feel right. Upon further questioning, she still claimed innocence, but volunteered that some of the women in the office maybe deserved something bad, and she could understand why someone might do something.

Why might that be? we asked. Well, she told me, "People who s*** on other people might deserve to get s*** on." And once that was out, it all spilled out: she'd had a particularly bad day with a boss who had been treating her poorly, in her opinion, for years, and she'd just felt the need to do something, and in the heat of the moment, that's what she'd done—to give them back what they'd given her, she said. She was utterly embarrassed now.

Call it temporary insanity.

All I can say is, if you find yourself taking a lot of "s***" at your job, this is not the way to give it back.

TIPS

Washing Your Hands of It

This seems like a good place to remind you that the benefits of washing your hands go well beyond cleaning up any incidental contact with bathroom leftovers. Over the course of a normal day, you probably touch doors, elevator buttons, handrails, seats on public transit, and hundreds of other things that other people have touched with their possibly germ-laden hands (or other parts). Throw in papers, keyboards, and so on, that somebody coughed or sneezed on. . . . Wash your hands regularly. It's the simplest germ avoidance and illness prevention there is.

To make sure your hands are thoroughly clean, the Centers for Disease Control recommends scrubbing for twenty seconds. That's about as long as it takes to sing "Happy Birthday" twice. But do your coworkers a favor and don't sing it out loud!

MEMO TO MANAGEMENT

It's increasingly common to see hand sanitizer dispensers around offices. These are a great idea—not just to address bathroom issues, but to minimize the germs being passed by contact with surfaces and objects. You can decrease the spread of seasonal colds and flu, and the impact on productivity when employees are sick, by giving employees every resource to prevent the spread of germs.

An employee we'll call Pat was in the process of a gender transition from male to female. This was a difficult time for Pat, as she went through the process of adapting to her new, preferred gender identity, a process that is all but impossible to accomplish in anything but a very public way if you work anywhere except at home alone.

It was also uncomfortable for Pat's coworkers, most of whom had never known a trans person, and many of whom were discomfited by the idea and the situation. Some of these employees taunted and mocked Pat about the transition, basically expressing their own discomfort by making things uncomfortable for Pat.

At a certain point in the transition, Pat explained to Human Resources that she felt far enough along in the process that it would be appropriate for her to use the women's restroom rather than the men's. While this would help keep her out of the eye of some of her male harassers, it also led to another problem: female employees complained about sharing a restroom with someone they had known as male and still considered not one of them.

We didn't have a unisex restroom available, which would have been one solution, so we had to handle the situation through tactful conversation with employees. It took time for the situation to settle down, and there will always be some people who aren't entirely comfortable about it, but we let our employees know that respecting each other, even in the face of discomfort or awkwardness, is paramount.

MEMO TO MANAGEMENT

Hiring an employee who has already made a transition from one gender to the other is fairly straightforward. There may be some logistical issues if the employment history is under two different first names, or if the employee is calling him- or herself by a name that isn't the one on his or her birth certificate or Social Security card, but that can be handled confidentially in the human resources department without other employees being the wiser.

Gender transition by an employee already in the workplace is a more challenging situation, but one that is becoming more frequent as awareness of transgender people in society is increasing and more transgender people are openly transitioning. The key to handling the situation is focusing on the person as an employee and a member of the team—whatever may change about this individual, the fact is that he or she is still a valued employee, colleague, and member of the team.

As with any employee issue, it's important to remain supportive and compassionate but to draw the line at bending over backward in ways that affect the ability of the company to go about its business. If the focus remains on doing the job, it's a bit easier to keep a personal matter of this sort from becoming the focus of everyone's attention and angst.

CASE FILE
Funky Time

There was a recurring problem in one of the restrooms: one of my colleagues found a note posted on the inside of the door of each stall in the ladies' room.

To whoever it is who comes in here every day between 4:30 p.m.-5:00 p.m. and funks this place up to high heaven:

Please be aware that this is not your home. Everyone has to share this bathroom. We don't want to gag on the stench you leave behind nor do we want to see your poop trails in the toilet on a daily basis. Your behavior is absolutely disgusting.

Either start bringing some heavy-duty air freshener in here with your smelly self and make sure you flush until ALL your poop is gone from the bowl or please go find yourself another toilet to contaminate.

Well, I think that says it all. Certainly makes you want to use a different restroom, doesn't it?

My colleague's concern was exactly that even if a visitor didn't arrive during the apparently regularly scheduled funky time in that bathroom, seeing that note wouldn't exactly convey the best impression of our firm.

I had the notes removed from the bathroom, and our HR representative sent out a more diplomatic memo to the staff reminding them to be considerate of others when using the restrooms.

Here's hoping the offender saw the memo and got the message before someone spouted off on the stall walls again.

TIPS
Bathroom Etiquette

Someone should have taught you this long before now, but in case not:

- Use the toilet, not the area around the toilet, for your business. Nobody likes to have to navigate around your dribbles.
- If you leave a skid mark on the toilet seat, wipe it off. Someone else has to sit there after you.
- Flush! And check to make sure there are no souvenirs left behind. If necessary, flush again.

- Most women's restrooms have a receptacle for used feminine hygiene products. It's there for a reason. If you feel the need to announce to everyone that you're having your period, please don't do it by leaving tampons or pads in view. . . . In fact, if you feel the need to announce your period, suppress that need.
- Wash your hands when you're finished. I don't care if you "didn't really touch anything," your coworkers don't want to touch anything you've touched if you don't wash up.
- Put the used paper towels in the trash can. The floor or the general vicinity of the trash can does not count.

MEMO TO MANAGEMENT

The company may be responsible for supplying and maintaining the restrooms in your facility, or it may be the responsibility of the landlord or property management. In either case, it's important to the well-being and morale of your staff to make sure the premises are well stocked and in good shape.

If it's the building's responsibility and they are not providing adequate supplies—for example, I heard of a company where the feminine hygiene product dispenser was empty for months—you can address it with the management of the premises, but if they are not responsive, you may have to arrange to supplement supplies yourself and work it out with them at lease negotiation time. Improving on what is supplied by adding hand lotion, air freshener, and other amenities is a small investment that will yield a surprisingly large reward in terms of how employees feel about the workplace . . . and that, in turn, improves loyalty and productivity in the longer run.

While we are on the subject of bathroom courtesies, management should know that how employees treat and leave the restroom may be a good barometer of workplace morale. When employees do things like throw stuff around the restroom, cause intentional messes, and stop up toilets, it often means morale in the office is low. Biannual (blind) employee surveys are an excellent way to keep your finger on the pulse of employees' feelings about their jobs, the workplace, and upper-level management. A good, old-fashioned, anonymous suggestion box doesn't usually hurt, either!

CASE FILE
Black-and-White

You do things in the restroom that you wouldn't do out in public, and sometimes that leads people to say things in the restroom that they'd never say elsewhere in the office. News flash: your colleagues' ears don't stop working when they enter the facilities.

We had a manager who knew better than to express his racist opinions in meetings, but it was a different story in the men's room. He told a coworker that he wouldn't use a stall that had been used by an African American employee because, he said, "I'm afraid of what I might catch off the toilet seat."

What he caught was a stern reprimand and some sensitivity training.

CASE FILE
Watch Out Where You're Pointing That Thing!

Two male employees, whom we'll call Tom and Tim, had a bit of a disagreement in the hallway on the way to the restroom. It got heated and loud, and continued as they headed into the men's room. Before long, they were side by side at the urinal shouting each other down about whatever was at issue (the source of the argument was long forgotten in its aftermath).

Tom made a particularly forceful remark at Tim, who spun on him and got in his face to refute it. Tim had, however, been urinating at the time. As he fired his verbal fusillade at Tom, he fired something else at Tom's trousers.

Tom immediately zipped up and brought himself, his pants dripping with evidence (à la Monica Lewinsky's infamous blue dress), to the human resources department.

Tim was fired. There are some things that are just never okay.

TIPS
Conservation of Bodily Fluids

Your bodily fluids are your own. Spit, pee, whatever—keep it to yourself or dispose of it appropriately. Think of it this way: no matter how angry you are, you don't want to leave DNA evidence.

MEMO TO MANAGEMENT

Speaking of DNA: You are probably not going to do DNA testing to find out who peed on Tom's trousers or who has been leaving puddles on the bathroom floor . . . but your employees don't know that. You could do it if you really wanted to, and thanks to television crime shows, employees are well aware of it. The suggestion or threat that you will identify the culprit with CSI-like precision may be all it takes to stop the offensive behavior or elicit a confession.

One day, an employee returning to his car in the company's underground parking garage stumbled into something quite unpleasant—a pile of "number two" next to a pillar in the garage. He complained to the facilities manager, who assumed someone had brought a dog in to work.

A few days later, another employee made a similar discovery elsewhere in the parking lot, and facilities staff went to investigate. "Doesn't look like dog poop," someone remarked.

Garage security cameras had seen no sign of anyone walking a dog in the garage. Both piles of someone's business were near pillars where view from security cameras was obstructed, but in order to get to that location, a dog—owned or on its own—or a homeless person, or whatever, would have been seen. What we did see on the security camera footage were our own people—numerous employees coming and going, though no indication whether one of them might have been, um, going. A mystery.

And then it happened again. This was becoming a serious problem, not to mention a source of much company gossip. We arranged for security guards to circulate around the underground garage, watching for suspicious activity (like someone groaning while squatting) that might occur out of the view of the security cameras.

"KEVIN, DO HURRY UP – IF I'M LATE AGAIN WE'LL BOTH BE IN THE DOG HOUSE!"

Sure enough, a few days later, an employee was caught with his pants down—literally—in the act of leaving a surprise. When confronted, the perpetrator admitted what he had done—how could he not, when he'd been seen? He defended himself by claiming he had done it at previous jobs, without consequences, and explained that he felt a compelling need to "mark the territory" as his.

I'm just grateful he didn't feel the urge to mark the territory around his desk. We fired him. Who knows what territory he is staking his claim to now.

CASE FILE

A Pleasure to Work Here

I've had quite a few uncomfortable conversations with employees over the years, as you can guess from some of the stories I've shared in this book, but I think this was the all-time most awkward. An employee we will call Willy was making it a habit to, shall we say, pleasure himself in a stall in the men's room.

He wasn't discreet enough to wait until others weren't around, either. Several men in the workplace knew about it because so many had heard the telltale sounds of Willy's self-ministrations. Finally, someone brought it to the attention of management, and I was the lucky winner who got to explain to Willy that spanking the monkey, choking the chicken, basting the ham, engaging in safe sex, milking the snake, shaking hands with John Thomas, shining the shillelagh—whatever you want to call it, you don't do it at work.

CASE FILE
Work of Shame

At one company, we had a female employee, Lucy, turn up at the office early a few mornings a week wearing a cocktail dress or similar attire from the evening before. "I didn't have time to go home," she admitted. Then she would proceed to gather an array of toiletries and a change of clothes from her desk drawer (she must have kept an entire wardrobe there, for how frequently this was happening!), undress in the ladies' room, and give herself a sponge bath at the bathroom sink. She even washed her hair in the sink and used the hand dryer to blow-dry it! Finally, she would get dressed and apply her makeup before tidying up the counter, packing up the previous evening's attire, and reporting for duty.

Since Lucy was arriving early to allow time for her morning ablutions and showing up at her desk ready to work at nine o'clock, her activities weren't interfering with productivity. But for employees who came in before nine, either by choice or because they started earlier, and who stumbled on Lucy in the bathroom, half-clothed and monopolizing the sink area, it was becoming irritating. That and the sink drains were frequently clogged; they weren't made for hair washing.

The clogged drains led us to send a memo around asking employees to be careful what they put down the drains; no one had at that point reported Lucy's activity because she was a well-liked employee and tried to be considerate of others by wiping up any water she splashed around and making sure not to leave a mess. But the drain memo eventually led someone to mention to management that it was probably Lucy's hair washing that was causing the problem.

Someone suggested to Lucy that she might instead consider joining a local gym. Whether or not she chose to work out there, she would be able to avail herself of a proper shower, along with towels and a locker for her copious supply of personal care products.

TIPS

Remember: Your Mother Doesn't Work Here

And even if she did, it wouldn't be her job to clean up after you at the workplace.

Also, you don't live at the workplace. Even if it seems like you do, based on how much time and energy you spend at work, don't make yourself too much at home.

And definitely don't do anything at work that you wouldn't do in your own home. In fact, don't do anything at work you wouldn't want your mother to see or know about!

CHAPTER 8

When the Cat Gets Out of the Bag

So what happens when things reach the point of a human resources investigation?

I should say at the outset that, although I am a lawyer, this is general information and nothing in this book should be construed as legal advice. If you need legal advice, consult an attorney in your area who specializes in employment law. Note, too, that laws about employment matters vary from place to place, and even from industry to industry—if you're a government employee, for example, you are probably operating under a different set of rules than someone working in a fast food establishment. (But neither of you should spit in my food. Thanks.)

All that said, here's what you need to know.

Silence Is Golden

The primary rule of a human resources investigation is confidentiality.

Good luck with that in many workplaces.

Seriously, if you are involved in any way in an investigation—as the person who raised the issue, as the person being investigated, as a witness, or as the investigator—keep things under your hat. Not to say if you were harassed, for example, that you can't tell your spouse or family members about it, and certainly if it's a situation that requires legal counsel (we'll talk about that below) you can talk to your lawyer. But in the workplace, you should keep things to yourself. Gossip only complicates matters. People start to "remember" what they heard someone else say rather than what really happened, or take sides, or perhaps spread a damaging rumor that turns out to be false. Zip your lip outside the investigatory process.

Moreover, your company may very likely have a formal policy that prohibits discussing human resources investigations, with the penalty being dismissal. Even if the company doesn't have such a policy, chattering about a confidential personnel matter is not going to be looked upon kindly by your company's management.

Need to Know Basis

Human resources representatives will, of course, discuss cases and situations among their department as part of their staff meetings or in order to share or obtain further information. They will want to find out, for example, whether a similar issue has been brought to the attention of someone else in HR, or if other HR staff are aware of previous complaints about someone. If there is any possibility of legal liability, the company's lawyer or law firm may also be in the loop.

The situation will probably also be discussed with the supervisors of the parties involved—unless one of those supervisors is the subject of scrutiny, in which case HR may do more investigating before confronting that person. The reason supervisors are involved is that they may have additional information that bears on the case, and also so that they know why their people are being called away from their work to talk to someone in human resources.

Depending on how the company is structured, HR may also be required to report its activities and investigations to management who supervise HR and to other senior management. In some companies, all senior-level managers expect to be looped in.

That may be a lot of people. In theory, they should all be responsible for respecting the confidentiality of the investigation and the people involved. In practice, however, that isn't always the case. I heard of one company in which the CEO and the company lawyer discussed a confidential personnel matter in the elevator, oblivious to the presence of other riders, who included other employees of the company and a vendor. They didn't name names, but they sure set off a guessing game around the office.

Just because someone else may talk out of school, however, doesn't mean you should. Do you really want to be the subject of a *different* inquiry when someone's personal information is shared when it shouldn't have been?

When Do You Involve HR? From the Employee Standpoint

Let's back up a bit. When is it appropriate to take a problem to human resources in the first place? Ask yourself a couple questions.

Can I solve it myself?

If you can solve the problem yourself, you should. If someone who sits near you is using the speaker function for all his phone calls and it's distracting you from your work, talk to him politely, explaining the impact on your work, and suggest he close his door or use the handset. Sometimes, people don't realize the impact of their actions, and a friendly conversation is all it takes to make things right.

Is this a serious problem affecting work?

If you're running to HR to complain that you saw Joe Schmoe spill coffee in the kitchen and leave without wiping it up, you're going to be labeled a whiner and you're wasting a lot of people's time. Every office has someone who acts like the kindergarten tattletale, constantly running to management to point fingers over silly things. We had one guy coming to HR to complain whenever a nonhandicapped employee used the stall in the restroom designated for handicapped individuals. Don't be that guy (or girl).

Is your supervisor aware of the situation?

A lot of problems, especially ones related to the actual work—like someone not doing his or her job, or doing it in such a way that it hinders someone else doing his or her job—can be solved by the supervisors involved without going to HR. Take it first to your own manager. Plus, your boss doesn't want to find out from HR about a problem because you went running there instead of discussing it with him or her first. You just made the problem bigger, and that won't win you points. If your boss tries and fails to solve the problem, he or she can work up the line.

If the problem relates to another group/department, does their manager know about it?

There are always issues of territory: Is it your job to interfere in the business of other departments? If it's affecting your work, it's your problem, too, but that manager may be working on it. Determine with your manager whether it's appropriate to approach the other manager. He or she doesn't want to hear about problems from HR first, either.

Is this issue affecting the company, or is it just bothering you?

HR is interested in issues that affect the business, not things that annoy you. If you don't like someone, for example, that's not a business issue. Let's face it, in life you will have to deal with all kinds of people, and your job pays you money to do it, so put on your big boy/big girl pants and learn how to get along with people. You're not five. And if you act like you are, well, you probably shouldn't be earning a grown-up paycheck.

Is the problem your boss?

If your problem is with your manager, you might be able to address it with him or her first if you do so professionally, calmly, nonjudgmentally, and with specific examples and solutions. Sometimes, HR can be a good resource for such conversations, serving as a sanity check, advising you on how to approach your boss, or acting as a mediator if necessary. Use your judgment as to whether you can resolve this yourself first before you go to HR for help.

Explore other options before running to HR with your problem. They will be more responsive if they know you've thought the situation through and taken appropriate steps before seeking their help.

There are, however, some situations in which you should go immediately to human resources, and some that are likely to end up there in due course.

Do Not Pass Go: Go Directly to HR

- Instances of sexual harassment
- Any situation that may put you or your coworkers in physical danger
- Illegal conduct in the workplace or affecting the workplace
- Drug or alcohol use on the job
- Discrimination based on race, religion, or sex
- Accommodation needed for disability
- Violations of confidentiality—the company's, the customer's, the employee's—including data security breaches

It'll Be HR's Problem Eventually

- Disputes about salary, promotions, raises, evaluations
- Disruptive or abusive behavior toward other employees
- Violations of company policies
- Working conditions that affect many employees' ability to do their jobs

One of our employees, Cal, was gay. He worked in a cubicle next to a coworker who peeked over the divider at him almost every day to deliver a derogatory comment. He called Cal a "lazy faggot." He told Cal he was going to hell. He asked Cal, "Why are you walking funny? Oh, I know.

With what you probably did last night, I don't know how you can sit all day!"

Cal recognized this for what it was—sexual harassment—and came straight to HR. "We take this very seriously" has become a cliché, but it's the truth when it comes to sexual harassment. In some cases, the results of the investigation are ambiguous, but in this instance, Cal's workmate was loud, proud, and out the door. We had plenty of corroborating witnesses.

Know before You Go

If you're the one to bring a problem or issue to human resources, have all your ducks in a row. Often, workplace situations involve a lot of strong feelings, and being upset or angry may be perfectly reasonable. But what will help the human resources representative help you is information. If you have written evidence of a problem—an offensive email, for example—bring it. If possible, note when and where an incident happened and who else might have seen it so you can supply that information. If you believe there's a pattern of misbehavior—something goes missing regularly—be prepared to tell why you believe that to be the case.

That doesn't mean you have to go around playing *Law & Order*, gathering evidence and building your case. That's the job of the HR investigation. If the matter is serious enough to involve human resources, get there right away, while everything is fresh in your mind, with whatever information and evidence has led you to believe the matter serious enough for their involvement, and let HR take it from there.

Whatcha Gonna Do When They Come for You

Whether you're the person who brought the issue to HR, you're a witness or colleague being asked for information, or the person being investigated for an alleged misdeed, I have one piece of advice. It's important enough that I'm going to give it to you in all caps, so you can't miss it.

TELL THE TRUTH

The whole truth, and nothing but the truth. Anything else is going to backfire on you eventually, one way or another:

- If you did it, you'll get found out eventually. And then you're on the hook not just for the misdeed but for the lie. Fess up and take the first step toward making things right so you can have a chance of saving your job and reputation.
- If you're covering for someone for whatever reason, and the truth comes out, you're no longer just an uninvolved party who did nothing wrong. You're in trouble for lying.
- If you're trying to stay uninvolved by claiming not to have seen/known anything, and it turns out you did know or should have known, you'll be tagged either as dishonest or dumb. Cluelessness is not a highly valued employee trait.
- If you embellish charges in order to strengthen the charge against someone, that will come out in the course of an investigation, and your entire case may be dismissed as the product of your imagination.

"OKAY, YES...I **DID** LEAVE THE TOILET SEAT UP..."

- If the matter is serious enough to involve the courts, your lie may become perjury, and that's a crime.

So let me say it again: **Tell the truth.** HR personnel are not dumbasses. They'll figure it out if you're telling the truth. Or someone will. Nobody likes a liar. More importantly, nobody wants to hire a liar.

The investigator is also assessing your overall credibility—not just whether you're being honest, but whether you are a reliable source of information. Try to keep your cool as best you can in what is no doubt a stressful situation. Tell your story clearly and accurately to the best of your ability. If you are not sure about something, admit that. Explain why you believe it to be the case. Don't wander off on tangents. In short, be professional. If you comport yourself like a sane, reasonable person whose story is consistent, who answers questions clearly and can supply information—evidence, documentation, witnesses, reasons for assumptions or claims—you will be seen as credible and your comments taken seriously.

HR ≠ BFF

Although the human resources staff will do their best to be fair to all parties in an investigation, their job is ultimately to protect the interests of the business. No matter how nice someone in HR may be, or how sympathetic the rep may seem, his or her ultimate accountability is to the company and its bottom line. If the company and its productivity is negatively affected, HR will take whatever action is needed to resolve that. Niceness is not necessarily part of that equation.

Also, the HR rep is not your therapist. Take your personal troubles elsewhere.

Privacy Is an Illusion

In the course of an HR investigation—as we've seen in several of our case files—your electronic communication may be monitored. Don't say anything in email you wouldn't say out loud. Know also that your past electronic activities are fair game, too. You may think things have been deleted, but IT staff can often recover things you thought were ancient history.

There's a trend in many industries toward open-plan offices. As we all share (less) space and work more closely (tightly packed), it's harder to keep things under your hat. If you're in a cubicle or open area, others are likely to hear your conversations. If the HR staff work in a similar setting, they may be sharing unwittingly. If a matter is sensitive, it's not inappropriate to ask for a private conversation.

MEMO TO MANAGEMENT: CONDUCTING THE INVESTIGATION

Do:

- Assure confidentiality. Not just in content, but in the conduct of the investigation. If the HR rep who never leaves his office is seen working his way through a department in a series of closed-door conversations, tongues will wag. Discretion is job one.
- Interview all parties and witnesses promptly. The longer you wait, the more time there is for details to be forgotten or recollections to change.

- Document the investigation thoroughly. This is especially important if there is likely to be any dispute about the outcome, or if legal action—by company or employee—is a possibility.
- Be honest with employees. Nothing is helped by giving false assurances or making empty threats. Model the honesty you expect from your employees.

Don't:

- Send people back to write things down. People tend to get creative when asked to write things out after the fact. Events may, intentionally or not, get edited to favor the person reporting when they go back to recount things in writing.
- Play favorites. There are some people you trust—because they have a good track record, or are good performers, or are easy to work with—and some you don't—because they have been in trouble or been difficult before or are cranky or complainers. Set those preconceptions aside when an investigation is under way. The nice guy or top employee who is considered above suspicion and uses that as cover for breaking rules may get away with something that will blow up later. Similarly, the pain-in-the-butt may actually be right. Give everyone a fair shake.
- Brush it under the rug. There may be pressure—overt or subtle—to let certain matters slide or to make a particular assessment about a situation because to do otherwise would reflect poorly on someone, or bring bad press, or simply be an issue that top management doesn't want to address. If

> there is a genuine violation—of law, particularly, as this kind of thing has a habit of occurring in discrimination cases, for one—the consequences of knowingly ignoring or dismissing it are more serious than if it had never been investigated. Even if it's more minor, such as a violation of company policy, consistently ignoring infractions undermines your ability to enforce rules when you need to.

Case Closed

What should you expect to hear after an HR investigation? Because there are often a lot of people to be interviewed, or the HR department may simply be (like everyone) overworked and understaffed, these things take time. But eventually, the case will be closed, one way or another.

If you're the subject of the investigation, you will, of course, be told whether you were found to have done something wrong because your supervisor or HR representative will tell you what the consequences are: what you have to do differently, what remedies you might have to deliver, whether you still have a job. Or, if you've been cleared of misconduct, the HR representative should inform you of that as well so you can get on with your life.

However, if you are not the subject of the investigation, the investigator is not obligated to tell you the outcome. If you are the person who raised the issue, as a courtesy, you may be told when the situation has been resolved. What you'll be told about specifics will depend on the situation: remember, if there are other people involved, their confidential personnel records are not your business. Human resources and legal staff will make their judgment about what to tell you based on the situation.

For example, if you were threatened by another employee, and that employee is being fired, you'd probably be told that so that you know the matter is concluded and you can feel safe again at the job.

But if you reported one of the, shall we say, colorful bathroom episodes we talked about in an earlier chapter, and didn't know who did it, HR may not feel it appropriate, in the interests of employee relations, to tell you who the poopmonster was. Just keep using the hand sanitizer.

Legal Eagles

People often ask me whether they should get a lawyer if they're accused of workplace misconduct.

If you're accused of something illegal, the police are likely to be involved, and your rights are defined by the law. You have—as you know if you've ever seen any cop or crime show—the right to an attorney, and if you're being charged with a crime, you would be wise to consult one immediately.

If it's not a criminal matter, you don't need to run out and get a lawyer. In most situations, that's overkill and an unnecessary expense. It's also like bringing a gun to a knife fight—you've now raised the stakes beyond what they were, making the situation much more confrontational.

Threatening to sue the company is similar—you've just raised the stakes. If the company lawyer wasn't involved before, he or she may be now. And we have all known the employee who accompanies every minor complaint with, "You know, my son/sister/nephew-in-law's cousin is a lawyer. . . ." If you think threatening legal action in that way makes people take you more seriously, think again. It just makes you more difficult. Maybe being difficult *is* warranted by the circumstances—but you had better be sure of that. And you best be prepared to deliver on that threat of legal action, which can get expensive. Remember, you're one person with one salary. Depending on the size of the company, they may have a lot of lawyers and very deep pockets. Be sure it's worth it before you escalate.

Discriminating Advice

What about cases of discrimination? If you have reason to believe you have been discriminated against, you should research your rights (which may vary, depending on your state, whether you are employed in government, etc.). Before you can file a lawsuit for any type of discrimination covered by most laws enforced by the federal Equal Employment Opportunity Commission, you are required to file an EEOC Charge of Discrimination. Visit the EEOC website (www.eeoc.gov) for more information and guidance in that process.

The process is different for government employees, but the same site can help you get started.

If you fear that raising the issue will cost you your job, a Charge of Discrimination can be filed on your behalf by another individual or—as is more common—by an organization. Associations advocating for and supporting the needs of various groups are often at the forefront of pursuing discrimination cases for their membership.

A caveat, though: just because you are [fill in the blank], and the person who isn't got the job, promotion, or whatever, doesn't mean you have been the victim of discrimination. There are a lot of reasons why that person might have been selected ahead of you. Ask why you were passed over, and make sure it's not simply that the other person had more qualifications or experience. Then use that information to make yourself a stronger candidate for the next opening.

CASE FILE

Colorful Remarks

Otis was a manager who had an issue with the back office area of his company. He complained to a colleague about it. His colleague wasn't aware of a problem and asked Otis what he thought was wrong. "Too many black people," Otis replied. "They don't work hard enough."

Needless to say, that kind of remark is unacceptable. (It was also completely untrue.) Otis was called on the carpet for attitude adjustment. His remark was damaging not only to morale and work relationships but also potentially opened the company to a lawsuit.

In a case of discrimination, the burden is on you to prove that your race/religion/sex/whatever was a factor, i.e., that you weren't selected because of that. In rare cases, that's straightforward: someone tells you they don't want to hire or promote someone like you. A generation or two ago, it wasn't uncommon for job seekers to be told outright: "We don't really feel a black person is the right face for our company" or "Our customers aren't really ready to trust a woman selling our product." But in this day and age, that kind of explicit discrimination is rare. People like Otis are vanishing.

Discrimination can be challenging to demonstrate, especially because it may not be overt or even conscious: nobody in the company *decided* to promote only straight white men. People sometimes choose people like themselves out of habit and comfort and may be genuinely stunned to hear that they may not have been evenhanded in their decisions.

In order to make your case, if you're satisfied that you have one, you may have to prove a pattern of discrimination; that it's not just you who was passed over, but highly qualified minorities have consistently been passed over in favor of less qualified nonminorities. This isn't easy. Seek expert advice before pursuing a discrimination claim.

Where do you go for that advice? A good first step is to talk with an organization that advocates for members of your group because they will understand your issues. Organizations like the NAACP (www.naacp.org), whose mission includes the elimination of racial discrimination; GLAAD (www.glaad.org), which works on behalf of lesbian, gay, bisexual, and transgender people; or NOW (www.now.org), whose focus is women's issues, have local chapters that can direct you to good resources for information. And if it seems that you might have a case, you will want to discuss the situation with an attorney experienced in employment discrimination cases.

CASE FILE
Seeds of Discontent

Discrimination usually means that choices about employment—hiring, raises, promotions, opportunities, etc.—are based on something other than performance. Another form of discrimination is harassment of employees because of their race, sex, or other attribute; that's called "a hostile work environment."

One white employee had issues with sharing the break room with African American employees. His method of expressing that was to leave a slice of watermelon on the counter or table every day.

When confronted, he feigned innocence, saying, "I just thought they liked watermelon." He had, however, made his views known to other white colleagues who didn't share his bigoted viewpoint.

We don't usually fire people for a first offense of this type if it doesn't affect our business directly. There's more to be gained in the long run by trying to educate the person and change his attitude by showing him why the behavior is wrong, how it affects coworkers and the company, and helping him see others as individuals rather than stereotypes.

TIPS

Protected Classes

Discrimination based on the following groups—"protected classes"—is prohibited under federal law:

- Race
- Color
- Religion
- Sex (including pregnancy)
- National origin
- Age (40 or older)
- Disability
- Genetic information

Note that sexual orientation is at this writing not a protected class under federal law. There may, however, be state or local protections in place.

CASE FILE
Dumb and Dumbest

Susan was a call center employee with a hearing impediment. We were satisfied that she was able to do her job, but that didn't keep two of her colleagues from subjecting her to verbal abuse because of her disability. They were careful to keep it on the downlow when supervisors were in range, so it was her word against theirs.

Susan decided to gather evidence by bringing a tape recorder to work. What we heard when she brought those tapes to us was appalling.

While on the phone with a customer, the two troublemakers could be heard saying, "That dumb b**** can't hear what is being told to her, so why bother being on the phone anyway." During the same call, one of them said, "Crawl over here on your knees and we'll show you what you're good at."

That was a two-fer: harassment based on her disability and sexual harassment. We had no trouble firing both of the offenders.

TIPS
Let's Go to the Tape

Call center employees are routinely recorded for quality control purposes; you've probably heard the recorded disclaimer to that effect while waiting for the next available representative. Secretly recording interactions in the workplace, though, can be dicey from a legal standpoint. Laws differ from state to state. Get legal advice before going too far.

MEMO TO MANAGEMENT: DODGING THE DISCRIMINATION BULLET

It's not difficult to protect yourself from charges of discrimination. Keep the following in mind:

- Be clear and explicit about qualifications and criteria for hiring, promotion, raises, etc. If the job description says the applicant must have three years of experience with Photoshop and the candidate who was turned down only has two years, it's hard for him or her to argue that your decision was based on anything except qualifications.
- Use those qualifications and criteria. If you decide you really want to promote someone with a different skill set than the one you originally told potential promotees, it's natural that they might think the decision was based on something other than qualifications. If you have to make a change midstream in what you're looking for, give every candidate an opportunity to compete based on those criteria.
- Be willing to answer reasonable questions. "We went in another direction" is open to a lot of interpretations, but "the other candidate communicated more effectively" makes it clear the decision was based on preparedness for the job. It also gives the applicant more information about what he or she can do in order to be a more competitive candidate for a future opening.

- Assess your workforce overall. Looking at the big picture will help you identify unconscious trends. If, for example, it seems like women never rise in a certain area of the company, it's worth examining whether suitable female candidates are being overlooked at promotion time. You don't need binders full of women—you just need to make sure there are no patterns of omission.
- If you do see patterns, examine what you can do to change that. Should you increase your recruiting at events that focus on groups that are underrepresented in your company? Maybe you see that there are few people of color in your company. Is that because potential candidates don't know about job opportunities in your company? A diverse workforce is an asset in serving a diverse community of customers or clients—and a protection against the appearance of discrimination.

No Big Payday

By the way, don't expect to hit the jackpot by suing for discrimination. The law seeks to make things right by putting you in the position you'd be in if the discrimination hadn't happened. That might mean giving you the promotion or back pay to cover the increase you were inappropriately denied. You might be able to get the other party to pay your attorney's fees and court costs if you win. But if you have the idea you'll sue for discrimination and land on Easy Street . . . wrong turn, buddy.

I Can Say Anything! You Can't Stop Me!

People fling "free speech" around with the idea that the First Amendment to the Constitution means you can say whatever you want, wherever and whenever you want, and anyone who tries to stop you is violating your civil liberties.

Wrong.

Here is what the amendment says:

> Congress shall make no law respecting an establishment of religion, or prohibiting the free exercise thereof; or abridging the freedom of speech, or of the press; or the right of the people peaceably to assemble, and to petition the Government for a redress of grievances.

Read those first five words carefully. The only people who can't restrict your speech are the members of Congress in their lawmaking capacity.

Can your boss tell you to take down that campaign poster or shut up about the company? Yep. Nothing to do with the First Amendment.

Now, to be fair, there is a complex history of legal decisions around what an employer can or can't do with respect to an employee's speech. But the bottom line is that while Congress can't make laws restricting your speech, lots of other people can put a gag on you.

So if you were thinking of deriding your company's products at the top of your lungs from the sidewalk out front, under the assumption that the company can't fire you because of the First Amendment, well, you'll have plenty of time to reconsider during your impending unemployment.

The Bottom Line

Allegations of workplace misconduct are serious business. The investigations are both important and sensitive in nature. If you are involved in any such scenario, tread lightly, proceed with caution, and communicate with sincerity.

If all else fails, you may want to duck and take cover!

CHAPTER 9

Employees Behaving Better

The benefits of working in an office, other business, or corporate environment go far beyond paychecks, health insurance, and retirement plans. Being part of a team can be a powerful thing, a source of creative and personal fulfillment. But surviving—and thriving—in the corporate minefield takes more than just common sense and good intentions. Whether you're an employee, manager, or human resources specialist, forewarned is forearmed. Use the cautionary tales and advice in this book to help keep you from being the next cautionary tale in your own office!

In that regard, there are at least five things I'd like you to take away from this book. These five lessons will help you get along better—and get ahead—in your workplace.

Lesson 1: It's All About the Benjamins

Yes, there are lots of things you—and your colleagues, and your employer—get out of a job besides money to pay the bills. Work can give you new skills, pride in a job well done, opportunities for personal development, new friends, and a wealth of experiences. (Not to mention witnessing enough craziness to write a book!) Those are great personal goals, and if you are fortunate enough to get all of that out of your job, that's a wonderful thing.

But your company does not exist for or survive on your personal fulfillment. Businesses go into operation in order to make money. Even nonprofits exist for a purpose separate from their employees' personal goals: they need to make money to support a particular cause or mission.

Therefore, if you contribute to the success and profitability of the organization, you are an asset. If you don't, you're a liability. And the goal of any balance sheet is to maximize the assets and minimize the liabilities.

Does terrorizing good employees contribute to the company's success? No, it drives good people away and can, in extreme cases, lead to expensive legal entanglements. Does making your coworkers miserable contribute to the company's success? Nope. Just distracts everyone from getting their jobs done.

If you're looking for personal fulfillment in a job, you may well find it, depending on what constitutes fulfillment for you. You have to try to make a good match between your goals and your company's. But always remember (despite whatever airy-fairy pronouncements you might get from an HR department tasked with improving morale), from the company's point of view, your satisfaction is only valuable as it contributes to the bottom line.

MEMO TO MANAGEMENT

That doesn't make all companies cutthroat, by any means. There are plenty of companies that have demonstrated that treating employees well leads to better employee retention, less expense to train new people, and positive attitudes both in the workplace and toward customers and clients. If you're in management, keep that in mind: happy people do better work. You, too, can contribute more to your bottom line by making sure you align people's personal goals and your professional needs.

Lesson 2: No Employee Is an Island

You don't work in a vacuum. Heck, even if you are self-employed, hunkered down in a cabin in the middle of a desert island with only the local wildlife for company, sending your work by carrier pigeon out to the world, somebody is interested in that work and presumably paying you for it.

Most of us are far from that desert island. We work with other people, lots of them. Each of those people is a human being, owed the same respect and consideration you would want. (Yes, they may not always give you that respect and consideration. Like your parents probably told you when you were a kid, just because everyone else jumps off a cliff doesn't mean you should jump off the cliff, too.)

There are a couple ways in which you can make your work life better by remembering you're not the center of the universe. The first is simply respecting the shared space. Clean up behind yourself because other people have to work/eat/function there. Don't belt out show tunes in your cubicle; other people are trying to hear themselves think. (Muttering darkly in a low tone—also distracting.) Show respect for your coworkers by respecting the place you all have to inhabit.

Even more valuable, think about other people's work needs. You'd be surprised—or maybe you wouldn't—how often people are completely oblivious to what happens before the work comes to them and after it leaves their hands. If you take the time to find out what the person ahead of you in the workflow does, how they do it and why, and the same for the person after you, you'll make better decisions about your own work and contribute more effectively to the overall workflow.

It comes down to another message you probably got as a child: Do unto others as you would have others do unto you.

MEMO TO MANAGEMENT

Isolation is the enemy of productivity. If you can find ways to facilitate positive employee communication, you'll reap the benefits.

If you have a company newsletter or blog or companywide meetings, use them to highlight what different departments or business groups do and how and why they do that. If employees in all areas, at all levels, understand the entire process and the reasoning behind things, they will be more apt to get behind your mission.

A friend who works in publishing told me about inviting a sales manager to talk to the editorial and production people involved with a particular book about why the book was being rushed to press (causing great pressure on the entire team). Once everyone understood the impact of the potential success of the book, they stopped complaining about the tight schedule and found solutions that would meet the sales needs.

Information helps everyone work together more effectively. Share it, don't hoard it.

Lesson 3: Keep Your Private Life Private

Colorful adventures, peccadillos, and day-to-day troubles are best checked at the door when you come to work. If you're worrying about whether you remembered to pay that bill or whether your daughter did her homework, you're not focused on the work in front of you, and you will make mistakes. When you make mistakes on the job, the consequences range from the minor—you or somebody else has to fix the mistake or do it over, which isn't good for your reputation or advancement in the company—to the major—your error is costly to the company or endangers other employees or the customers using your product.

If you're able to do the same on the converse side—let work go when you walk into your home—you'll benefit from that as well. Focus on family, household, friends, and other activities after hours, and you'll be fresher and more prepared when you get back to the workplace.

Then there's chat; if you spend all day, every day, regaling coworkers with your nighttime adventures on the club circuit, they may tire of the distraction enough to raise the issue with a manager. A particularly resentful colleague—or one who has it in for you for some other reason—may use the information against you in a more damaging way—he or she might tell your boss you're not pulling your weight because all your clubbing means you come in hung over or even drunk or high.

Sharing personal information at work can have other consequences, too. We are cautioned about putting too much information out on social media about our children, lest those intent on harm use it to gain access to our kids. But long before Facebook and Twitter and even the internet existed, there were parents who shared vast quantities of family information with people they didn't know very well. Do you really want every Tom, Dick, or Harry who happens to have a job at the same place as you to know where your kids go to school and when their birthdays are? Not to say you can't ever talk about family or personal matters at work, but being discreet and limiting the amount of such talk is probably advisable.

TIPS

Friend Request

What do you do if a coworker or boss wants to friend you on Facebook or the like? If you are friends with that person outside of work, maybe you'll feel comfortable accepting. But if you don't want to accept and are concerned that rejecting the invitation will be taken amiss, you can always explain that you use Facebook primarily for communicating with family members in order to smooth things over. And if you do accept the invitation, I strongly recommend you familiarize yourself with the privacy settings of your chosen social media and make use of them. Remember, too, that some social media, e.g., Twitter, are inherently public. You may think your ancient, gray-haired boss doesn't know what Twitter is, so you're perfectly safe dissing him there. You'd be surprised how many graybeards tweet. And even if he doesn't, what's to keep someone else from sharing your tweet with him?

MEMO TO MANAGEMENT

Although there is a movement to have employees stay connected constantly, keep in mind the need for employees to relax and refresh so they come back to work with clear heads. Some of the best ideas come to the forefront when you're not thinking about the problem; give your employees the chance for that to happen.

Making sure your employees have the opportunity to relax will also make them more effective on the job. You'll also see less burnout, which means you'll have the opportunity to retain the people in whom you've invested training and experience. And that will save you money in the long run.

Moreover, if employees have no opportunity to focus on personal matters—whether it be talking to a child's teacher or dealing with a major financial issue—outside of work, those things will creep into the working day out of necessity. That sets a precedent for other employees that it's okay to take care of personal business during the workday, and pretty soon everyone's productivity is diminished as they try to do two jobs—the one you're paying for and the work of managing home and family—during the workday. In the long run, it makes good business sense to draw a line between work time and personal time and respect that line.

Lesson 4: You Can't Win 'Em All

Sometimes, we herald people for their "uncompromising" dedication to something. There are certainly things that should never be open to compromise—things affecting safety, for example—but in many things, compromise is key to getting anything done. Digging your heels in and refusing to move will just mean you're left behind.

And sometimes you just have to give in.

There are going to be times in your working life when you can't get anyone else to see your point of view. While sticking to your guns may seem like the right thing to do, after a while, everyone else will be sick of hearing you rant about the same thing. Step back, take a breath, and let things go. In time, you may be able to collect more evidence to support your position and win people over. Oh, and if you do eventually win—say, if things went badly awry because they didn't do what you suggested, and now they are going to take your advice—be gracious in victory. You don't win friends by screaming, "I told you so! You should have listened to me!"

No matter how right you are, in business, the boss gets to win. You may not like it, but that's the way hierarchy works.

If you know your boss is driving the company train straight off the rails, and he or she is not willing to hear it, you won't win yourself any goodwill by harping on it. At that point, you have to decide for yourself how serious an issue this is: Will you ride along, knowing the decisions being made are the wrong ones, because you need the job and don't have a lot of options right now? Will the consequences affect the boss or will they affect you? Knowing that the boss and you are always going to be working at cross purposes, can you still contribute effectively? If not, it's time to move on.

If you differ with a boss or coworkers on minor issues, compromise on at least some of those issues. Nobody is going to want to work with you if every little thing is a fight. And that will affect your performance reviews, raises, and ability to advance. In short: don't be a pain in the butt.

MEMO TO MANAGEMENT

Employees will be much more likely to go along with a controversial decision if they understand the reasoning behind it. Not to say that management should have to justify everything to employees, but if an employee or a group of employees is opposed to or confused by a choice made by management, you can defuse any negative behavior (and potential loss of good employees) with a willingness to discuss the "why" behind it. Once employees have the background about the situation or the information that influenced the management decision—information they didn't have—you may win them over and get their enthusiastic support. And even if minds are not changed, openness to conversation about the matter will create an atmosphere of collaboration. Employees will feel that they are part of the team, not just cogs in the machine who are simply told what to do.

Lesson 5: Doing the Work Is Less Work Than Pretending to Do the Work

It never fails to amaze me how many people there are who spend vast amounts of energy avoiding work—when they could have done the work they were avoiding in less time, with less energy expended.

People make up dozens of excuses why something isn't done. They find make-work tasks to do so that they won't have to work on the thing they don't want to work on. They bustle around talking to other people instead of doing their actual work. They avoid bosses or colleagues so they won't have to admit they haven't done the work—I've seen people so good at hiding that they ought to consider careers in the witness protection program! They will change the clock on their computer to make it look like an email was sent at a different time, they will falsify documents, they will hide things in other people's offices—all that effort not to do work is a lot of work!

And eventually, the work is going to have to be done. So, as the ad says, just do it.

Some employees think that if they make it hard to get them to do something they don't want to do, eventually others will take the path of least resistance and just do it themselves or have someone else do it. That might work once or twice, but before too long, colleagues will resent doing your work and management will notice that they are having to reassign your work . . . and the question will be: If this person doesn't do the job, why do we need him/her?

The answer to that one is pretty obvious.

MEMO TO MANAGEMENT

Beware that last one—the employee who makes it so difficult to get him or her to do something that you routinely assign the work to someone else. Sometimes it's subtle: the person does the work, but does it badly, or in a roundabout way, or takes a long time about it. He or she will be positive, pretend to be receptive to criticism or direction, or will claim to be focusing on doing the job perfectly.

If you find yourself thinking, "I'll give it to Jane, because it's too much work to get John to do it in time," that's a red flag. Look closely at why you feel that way. If you feel like you don't have the time or energy to deal with a certain employee, it's probably time for a conversation with that employee about how he or she does the job. Making the employee aware that you realize what's going on may be enough to solve the problem.

I hope these five lessons will help you be happier and more productive (and therefore more successful, with many raises and opportunities to advance) in your work. And as for all the lessons by example throughout this book:

Try not to be that guy/girl.